Step-by-step
CRAFTS
for
CHILDREN

KINGFISHER
Larousse Kingfisher Chambers Inc.
95 Madison Avenue
New York, New York 10016
This edition produced for Advanced Marketing Services, Inc.
5880 Oberlin Drive, Suite 400
San Diego, CA 92121

First edition 1996
2 4 6 8 10 9 7 5 3 1

ISBN 0-7534-5039-9

Editor: Deri Robins
Designer: Ben White
Illustrator: Jim Robins
Photographers: Rolf Cornell (SCL Photographic Services),
Steve Shott, Steven Sullivan
Cover design by Terry Woodley
Printed in Hong Kong

Step-by-step CRAFTS for CHILDREN

- **JEWELRY** Sara Grisewood
- **COLLAGE** Jim Robins and Philip Steele
- **PAPIER MÂCHÉ** Deri Robins
- **KITES** David Michael
- **CARDS** Charlotte Stowell
- **BOOKS** Charlotte Stowell

Kingfisher

CONTENTS

MAKING JEWELRY
8 – 44

COLLAGE
45 – 82

MAKING KITES
83 – 120

PAPIER MÂCHÉ
121 – 158

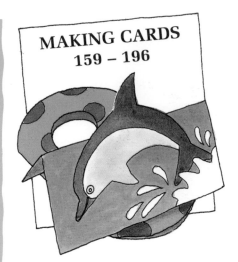

MAKING CARDS
159 – 196

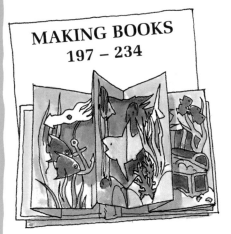

MAKING BOOKS
197 – 234

MAKING JEWELRY

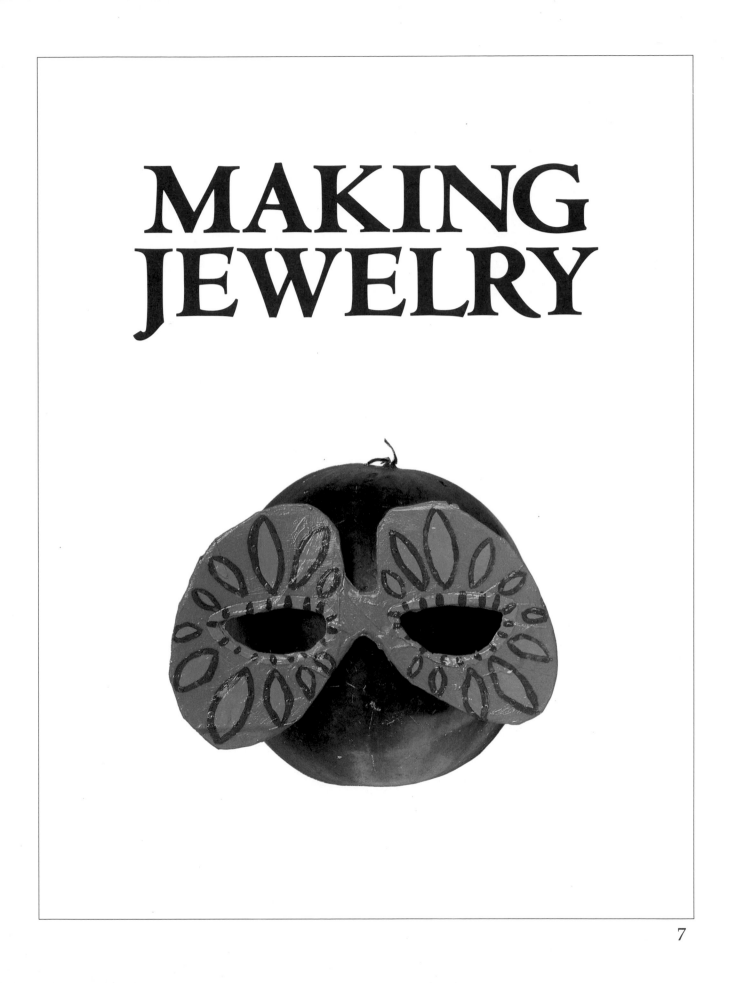

WHAT YOU NEED

You don't need expensive equipment or materials to make jewelry. You can use shells, felt, and leaves, as well as homemade papier-mâché and salt dough. Read all the instructions before you start to make sure that you have everything you need.

Paint

Varnish

Flour

Special Things

Findings are the special fastenings used to make jewelry. Necklaces can be tied with a knot, but you'll need findings for pins and earrings.

Craft stores sell findings, as well as beads, sequins, and fake gemstones.

Paper clips are ideal for pendant hooks—just stick them into the jewelry before baking. For threading heavy beads, buy a strong thread, such as linen carpet thread.

Wallpaper paste

Rolling pin

Colored clay

Salt

SAFETY TIP
*Craft knives, needles,
and skewers are very
sharp. Ask an adult to
help when you use them.*

Tools of the Trade

You'll need scissors, a craft knife, glue (a safe but strong epoxy glue), a pencil, metal ruler, masking tape, sewing thread, and needles.

An ordinary knife, fork and spoon, and a rolling pin make ideal tools for modeling. Work on an old board. Bake beads on metal skewers.

Buy colored clay, such as Fimo. Keep paper and wallpaper paste on hand for papier-mâché, and flour, salt, and water for salt dough *(see page 10).* You'll also need paints, brushes, and varnish *(see pages 12–13).*

String

Needle

Felt

Shells

Strong thread

Brush

Newspaper

Craft knife

Modeling tools

Findings

Scissors

Epoxy glue

Bought beads

9

Leaves

BASIC TECHNIQUES

Colored clay is ideal for making jewelry and doesn't even need a coat of paint. Other modeling materials, such as salt dough and papier-mâché, can be made at home very cheaply.

Making Salt Dough

Stir together $\frac{1}{2}$ cup of salt with 3 cups of sifted flour. Slowly add between $7\frac{1}{2}$ and 12 fl. ounces of warm water.

Mix together to make a soft dough. Knead until smooth, then leave it in a plastic bag for half an hour before using.

Bake your pieces at 340°F. Beads and pins take between $\frac{1}{2}$–$1\frac{1}{2}$ hours. Ask an adult to tap them—if they sound hollow, they are ready.

Most wallpaper pastes contain fungicide, which is poisonous. Always buy a nonfungicidal paste and follow the instructions on the package carefully.

Making Papier-Mâché

Old cereal boxes will make ideal cardboard bases for your jewelry. Cover your base with layers of torn newspaper dipped in wallpaper paste. The smaller the strips, the smoother your jewelry will be. Let the papier-mâché dry between layers.

Using Colored Clay

You can buy colored clay from craft and toy stores—it even comes in metallic and fluorescent colors! Always follow the instructions on the package before baking. Work on a board and clean your work surface before you change colors.

Finish off salt-dough and papier-mâché pieces by painting and varnishing them. Varnish also stops decorations from falling off and protects fragile objects, such as leaves—after all, painting isn't the only way to decorate your jewelry.

Paints and Brushes

Always let salt-dough jewelry cool and papier-mâché objects dry before painting. Apply a coat of white latex paint first so that you have a smooth, white surface to decorate. It will keep newsprint from showing through on your papier-mâché pieces.

Acrylic paints are best if you want really dazzling results, but poster paints give bright colors, too, and are much cheaper. Latex, acrylics, and poster paints are all water-based, so all you'll need to clean your brushes is plenty of water.

Keep a selection of brushes handy. A large, thick brush is best for the base coat, but you'll need finer ones for painting details, especially on homemade beads.

When you have lots of beads to paint, thread them on metal skewers. Rest the needle across an open shoe box, then paint. Leave the beads on the needle until they are all dry.

Using a cloth to rub gold paint on top of green will make your jewelry look like a valuable antique!

Tricks with Paint

After the latex paint, apply a base color. When this is dry, use a fine brush to paint a pattern on top.

Try smearing paint onto wood with your fingers. This gives an uneven and unusual stained effect.

Bits and Pieces

You can glue all sorts of daring decorations onto your jewelry. Use a strong epoxy glue or ordinary white glue.

Gems, natural objects (such as seeds), and even string can all be used as unusual surface decorations. The only limit is your imagination!

Varnishing

Give all your painted jewelry a glossy coat of polyurethane varnish. It makes the paint really shine and stops it from chipping.

When varnishing, make sure there is enough air in the room. Varnish can be dangerous if you breathe in too much of it. Always keep the window wide open.

BRILLIANT PINS

These pins will really brighten up a jacket or coat! We used colored clay for the balloon and the musical pins and added layers of clay to make raised patterns—this is called "relief" decoration.

1

2

3

Salt-dough Pins

Draw and cut out simple shapes on cardboard to use as templates for your pins.

Roll out a slab of salt dough to about $\frac{1}{3}$ inch thick. Put the templates on the dough.

Now cut around the templates. You can cut out holes for windows too, if you want.

4

5

6

To mark the edges of the windows or wheels, dig into the dough with a fingernail or knife.

Bake the pins in the oven. Leave them to cool, then paint and varnish the fronts.

Stick a finding to the back, using a strong glue. Let the glue dry, then wear your pin!

14

To make this hot-air balloon, you'll need to roll very thin layers of colored clay. Try not to smudge them!

Salt dough is just the thing for these chunky, colorful pins.

Musical Pins

1 Make templates for the guitar and keyboard. Place them on $\frac{1}{4}$-inch-thick colored clay and cut around them.

2 Cut out piano keys and the guitar trimmings and press into place. Mark piano keys and guitar frets with a knife.

3 Bake the pins in the oven. When they are cool, use a strong glue to attach findings to the back.

FLOWERS AND BOWS

Salt-dough flowers and bows make pretty pins. Bake all your pieces together, leave to cool, and then paint and varnish. Finally, glue findings to the backs. Brooches make wonderful presents—if you can bear to give these away!

Bows

Roll out some salt dough to $\frac{1}{4}$ inch thick. Then use a knife to cut a strip ($\frac{1}{2}$ in. x 6 in.), like a salt-dough ribbon.

small strip goes over the joint

Loop the strip into a bow, as if it were a ribbon. Join together wherever one layer overlaps another—just dab with water and press gently. Use an extra scrap to cover the center.

To make a bow-tie pin, cut out a basic bow-tie shape and a small rectangle (for the "knot") from salt dough. Stick the knot on with a dab of water.

Flowers

Make a cardboard template for the petals. Cut out about ten petals from salt dough.

Overlap the petals to make a circle. Dab with water and smooth the joints.

Press a blob of dough in the center of each flower to hide where the petals joined.

For another kind of flower, cut the base with a cookie cutter. Stick four diamond-shaped petals on top.

You can also make flowers by sticking four smaller petals on top of four larger ones.

RINGS AND THINGS

Papier-mâché is perfect for making fun, chunky jewelry. You can decorate rings with jewels made from scrunched-up tissue paper. Finally, use bright paints in different colors. Let each coat of paint dry before using a new color. Always make sure your bangles and rings are big enough to slide on and off your wrist and fingers easily.

1

Cut two strips of thin cardboard. Give one a wavy edge. Ask a friend to hold each strip around your hand and tape it together for you.

2

Cut narrower strips to make rings. Wrap them around your finger, so they slide off easily, then tape the ends together as before.

3

For a chunky bracelet, take six strips of newspaper and twist them together. Wrap this rope around your wrist and tape as before.

4 Cover the outside of all the pieces with three layers of papier-mâché. If you take the strips over the edges, you'll get a smooth finish.

5 Scrunch up tissue paper jewels for the rings. Tape them on and cover with a layer of papier-mâché to give a smooth finish.

6 Paint a white latex base and then use bold acrylics. Rub gold paint onto the chunky bangle *(see page 12)*. Finish off with a coat of varnish.

BEAD NECKLACES

Salt-dough beads look great threaded together with beads bought from craft stores.
Try making round beads, then go for new shapes, such as the Egyptian eyes. Mix different types together—string big, homemade beads with tiny colored glass ones.

1

Pinch off a small piece of salt dough and roll it into a ball in your palm.

2

Push each bead onto a metal skewer. Smooth each bead's surface.

3

Bake the beads on their skewers. Paint and varnish when cool.

Threading Beads

Take a length of strong thread. Tape down one end with masking tape (so your beads don't fall off), then thread on the beads with a needle. Peel off the tape and knot the ends of thread together. Feed the leftover thread neatly back through the beads.

Beads don't have to be round— these are shaped like Egyptian eyes! Push in a metal paper clip before baking and thread them by the hooks.

For a lucky charm, tie red ribbon to a spare Egyptian eye bead. Pin the ribbon on with a safety pin.

BEACHCOMBING

The beach is a treasure trove for jewelers! But shells can be tricky to drill, so it is usually easier to buy them with ready-drilled holes from a craft store. Show off the shells by trying out these different ways of threading.

Drilling

If you do want to use shells that you've collected yourself, ask an adult to drill holes in them for you. They will need to use a drill with a fine bit. Always wash the shells first.

Threading Shells

1 With some thread, tie about three shells to the middle of a leather thong. Try using a colored thong.

2 Thread a bead, then a shell, then go back through the bead. Leave a space before threading the next two.

3 Knot some string, thread on a shell, then knot again. Leave a space, then repeat with a bead.

Jazz up your necklaces with textured threads—try using string, leather thongs, or raffia.

Driftwood Pendant

Take a small piece of driftwood. Ask an adult to drill a hole in it.

Smooth the edges of your driftwood. To make your own sander, wrap fine sandpaper around a block of wood.

Stain the wood with paint *(see page 13)* and glue on coiled spirals of string. Thread onto heavy cord or string.

Shells look great threaded with sea-blue glass beads.

EARRINGS

You can wear earrings whether your ears are pierced or not. Craft stores sell clip-on earring findings as well as ones for pierced ears. Glue clip-ons to the back of the finished earring.

Pierced Ears

Findings for pierced ears have two parts. The hook is the part that goes through your ear. It slips onto the pin. There are two different kinds of pin—head pins and eye pins.

Hook

Eye pin

Head pin

Head pins are used for bead earrings. The head stops the beads from falling off *(see page 29)*. When the beads are in place, bend around the top of the pin with tweezers to make an eye for the hook.

Eye pins are used for papier-mâché or salt-dough earrings. They have an eye, but no head. Stick them into the earring so the eye pokes out at the top.

Salt Dough

Shape the salt dough—tiny fish and birds are easy and fun to do. Before baking, push in an eye pin. After baking, painting, and varnishing your earrings, slip the eye pin over a hook.

Papier-Mâché

1 Start with two shaped cardboard bases. Tape an eye pin to each base, so that the eye pokes out of the top.

2 Cover with two layers of papier-mâché. Make relief decorations with scrunched-up paper. When dry, cover with latex, paint, and varnish.

3 Slide the earring pin onto the hook by its eye. Squeeze the hook's wire so the pin won't slip off.

For a really snazzy special effect, rub on sparkling gold paint before varnishing.

PIRATE ATTACK!

You could wear this necklace of ghoulish skulls and clattering bone beads with a pirate costume for a party. The tiger beads were made in the same way as the skulls.

To make your skulls and bones look really rotten, mix a drop of yellow paint in with the white.

Thread the orange tiger beads with bright green ready-made beads.

1

With your hands, roll some salt dough into a sausage shape about 12 inches long. Cut into eight pieces.

2

Shape each piece to look like a bone. It's best to pinch the dough in at the middle of the bone and at both ends.

3

Roll eight balls of salt dough for the skulls. Squeeze in the cheeks. Use the end of a brush to make eye sockets.

4

Push all the beads onto metal skewers and bake in the oven. When cool, give everything a coat of white paint.

5

For extra ghoul-appeal, use black paint to make the skulls' eyes, noses, and mouths really stand out! Then varnish.

6

Thread the skulls and bones. Tie the ends of the thread to a button —it keeps the beads on as you work.

Bony Brooch

Join two bones in the middle with a dab of water, as shown. Press a skull on top.

Smooth the back of the brooch surface. Bake, paint, and varnish, then glue on a finding.

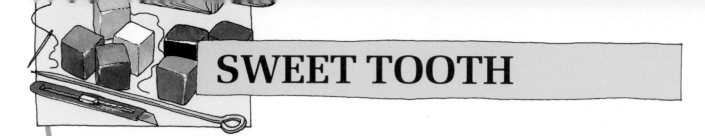

SWEET TOOTH

Use colored clay to make this delicious "candy" jewelry. Don't leave your beads lying around though—they look so realistic that someone might end up eating them!

1 Break off small lumps of clay. Roll into balls, then knock each one on your work surface to flatten the edges until you get a cube shape.

2 Make striped "candies" by rolling out layers of different-colored clays. Press them on top of each other, then cut into squares.

3 Roll some clay into a long sausage with your fingers. Wrap a new color around it and press gently. Smooth out where they join.

4 Cut the sausage shape into candy-sized beads. Make more in the same way, but change the thickness and cut to different lengths.

5 Push all your beads onto metal skewers and bake them in the oven, on a baking tray. Follow the instructions on the package carefully.

6 When the beads are all cool, thread them onto fine elastic, then knot the ends. You can make a necklace and a matching bracelet.

Make smaller beads for earrings. Use earring findings with head pins (see page 24).

PAPER JEWELRY

Rolled paper beads may look delicate, but the wallpaper paste makes them surprisingly strong. Try using all sorts of colored paper in lots of different thicknesses, as well as newspapers and old magazines.

For earring beads with a large hole, use an eye pin (see page 24), and bend back the pin with tweezers.

1

Make several cardboard templates. Rectangles make simple tube beads. To make oval beads, use a triangle. For fat beads use long templates. For long beads use wide templates.

2

Use the templates to cut out paper triangles and rectangles. To save time, fold the paper in an accordion and draw around the template. Then cut out lots of paper strips at once.

3

4

5

Coat both sides of each strip with paste, then roll around a skewer. Roll triangles from their base and rectangles from their short edge.

Slide the beads off the skewer and place on a wire rack to give the paste time to dry. There's no need to varnish the beads.

Thread the beads through their skewer holes, using strong cotton thread. Finish off by tying the thread with a double knot.

You don't have to thread all the beads through their skewer holes. If you thread through the top, they look spiky. Try bunching a group together like this.

31

BACK TO NATURE

Natural objects make delicate, unusual necklaces. Collect seeds and leaves outdoors, or raid the kitchen for bay leaves and melon seeds—anything you can find! You'll need to wash melon seeds, place them on paper towels, and leave them to dry in a warm place for a few days. A coat of varnish will give the bay leaves extra strength and shine.

1 Thread a needle. Knot the end of the thread and then push the needle through about ten melon seeds. Then thread a bay leaf.

2 Alternate rows of melon seeds and tree seeds or bay leaves. Tie a knot at the end to secure all the seeds and leaves.

3 Take a length of cord about $2\frac{1}{2}$ feet long. Position the string of seeds in the middle. Now cut another piece of thread and use it to tie one end of the row of seeds to the cord.

4 Use a double knot to attach the seeds to the cord, about every $\frac{3}{4}$ inch along, until you reach the end. Knot the ends of the cord and your necklace is ready to wear!

Always ask an adult before you gather seeds. Some of them are poisonous.

FELT FRUITS

Squares of felt come in just about every color of the rainbow. Felt is fabulous for making mouthwatering fruits like these.

Felt fruits look great pinned to clothes, bags, or floppy sunhats. Or why not display them in a mini fruit basket?

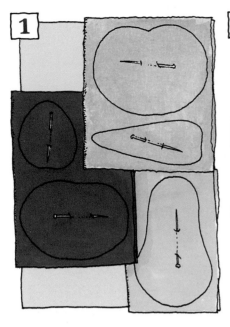

1 Draw templates for the tangerine, pear, carrot, tomato, and strawberry on paper. Cut them out and pin to scraps of felt.

2 Cut around each template twice. Sew the two halves of each fruit together, leaving a small opening.

3 Stuff each fruit with cotton balls, then sew up the gap. Cut out felt leaves and sew to the top of each fruit.

4 To finish, sew tiny colored beads to the strawberries. Push a tiny safety pin through the back of each fruit.

A Bunch of Cherries

Stitch around a small circle of red felt, then tighten the thread to pull the felt into a ball. Stuff the opening with cotton balls, then finish sewing up the cherry.

Cut thin strips of felt for the stems. Fold in half and stitch down the edge. Sew one to each cherry and pin together in bunches. Add stems to the strawberries, too.

GROOVY GLASSES

Make these swanky glasses for when you feel like some
larger-than-life dressing up! Design them in the
wackiest shapes you can imagine. Use bold,
vivid colors and paint on wild patterns.
For the sunburst glasses, build papier-
mâché sunrays across the eye holes.
Make sure you leave the slits wide
enough for you to see through.

1

Measure across your face and cut a piece of thin cardboard to this width. Hold it to your face and ask a friend to mark where your eyes and nose are.

2

Draw the outline of your glasses and cut them out carefully with a craft knife. Then measure and cut out a pair of arms for your glasses.

3

Make a hinge by taping the arms to the glasses with masking tape. Cover with about three layers of papier-mâché. Keep the arm hinges moving as the layers dry so you will be able to fold your finished glasses.

4

Coat the glasses with white latex, then paint a dazzling pattern in bright acrylic paints. Finish off your groovy glasses with a glossy layer of varnish.

MEGA MEDALS

Ever felt you deserved a medal? Well, now you can wear one that's big enough for everyone to see! The giant pocket watch is papier-mâché, too.

Hang the medals on lengths of ribbon and use gold string for the watch chain.

1

Draw the shapes onto thin cardboard and cut them out with a craft knife.

2¾ in.

2

Cover the cardboard bases with two layers of papier-mâché. For a raised watch face, tape on a smaller circle and cover with one more layer.

3

Paint and varnish your pieces. Use a darning needle to pierce a hole through the top of the watch for the chain. Reopen the hole after each coat of paint or varnish.

AZTEC JEWELRY

The Aztec people lived in South America hundreds of years ago and their goldsmiths were famous for their dazzling jewelry. Make your own glittering Aztec necklace and a matching ceremonial headdress, encrusted with gems. Finish off with a flourish of bright, colored feathers.

1

Cut out the cardboard necklace parts —you'll need a circle, two rectangles, and two triangles. Snip the tops of both triangles. Cut into the sides of one of the rectangles, as shown.

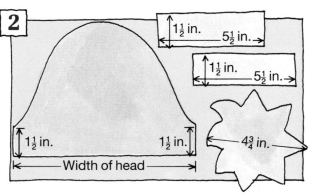

2

Measure the width of your head, then draw and cut out the headdress front, sides, and star. Bend the headdress so it fits the shape of your head, and then tape on the sides.

3

Cover all the shapes with three layers of papier-mâché. Tape scrunched-up paper to the headdress and star for raised decoration *(see page 25)*. Cover with a layer of papier-mâché.

4

Glue spirals of string onto the necklace pieces for relief decoration. Pierce holes with a skewer or a darning needle in the necklace pieces, headdress, and star as shown.

5

Cover the pieces with latex. Then paint the star and necklace pieces a shiny, Aztec gold. Use jade green for the headdress—the Aztecs loved jade.

6

When the headdress is dry, rub gold paint over the green with a cloth. Use a fine brush to paint extra details on all the pieces, then varnish.

7

Tie the necklace pieces together with short lengths of sparkling gold string. Use gold raffia at the top to hang the necklace around your neck.

8

Glue brightly colored feathers to the top of your headdress. Use wire to attach the star firmly on top, hiding the glue. Twist the wire at the back.

9

Glue bright felt streamers to the inside of the head-dress, so they flop over the top. To finish, glue on gems, sequins, and coils of string.

SHOWING OFF

Forget about boring old boxes! Why not show the pieces you have made on a crazy jewelry cactus? You can buy scrap wood for the base from a hardware store.

1

Ask an adult to saw a small block of wood (about 7 x 3 x ¾ inch) for a sturdy base.

2

Use tape to attach a cardboard tube, such as a toilet-paper roll, to the base.

3

Crumple some paper, stuff it into the tube, then tape it in place. This is for attaching your branches.

4

Cut out the branches from cardboard. The two large ones have two halves, so cut out four of these.

5

Stuff paper between the two halves of each large branch to pad it out. Hold the sides together with tape.

6 Tape all four branches to the cactus and cover everything with three layers of papier-mâché.

7 Give the cactus a latex base coat and then paint it bright green. Paint on yellow cactus spines, then varnish.

43

MORE IDEAS

By now you've probably realized that almost anything can be turned into jewelry. Here are a few more ideas you might like to try . . .

Wind some raffia around a cardboard bracelet. Sew embroidery thread in and out of the raffia, adding beads as you go.

Embroidery thread looks great braided. Tie the ends to a barrette, or knot them together to make a friendship bracelet. Add beads if you like.

For a choker, make a salt-dough heart with a hole in the middle. Use pink embroidery thread to sew the heart to a length of velvet ribbon. Glue on two Velcro squares for the fastening, or sew on snaps.

Use salt dough to make these cheerful key chain charms. Push in a paper clip before baking. After painting, slide it onto a key chain—you can buy them from craft stores.

COLLAGE

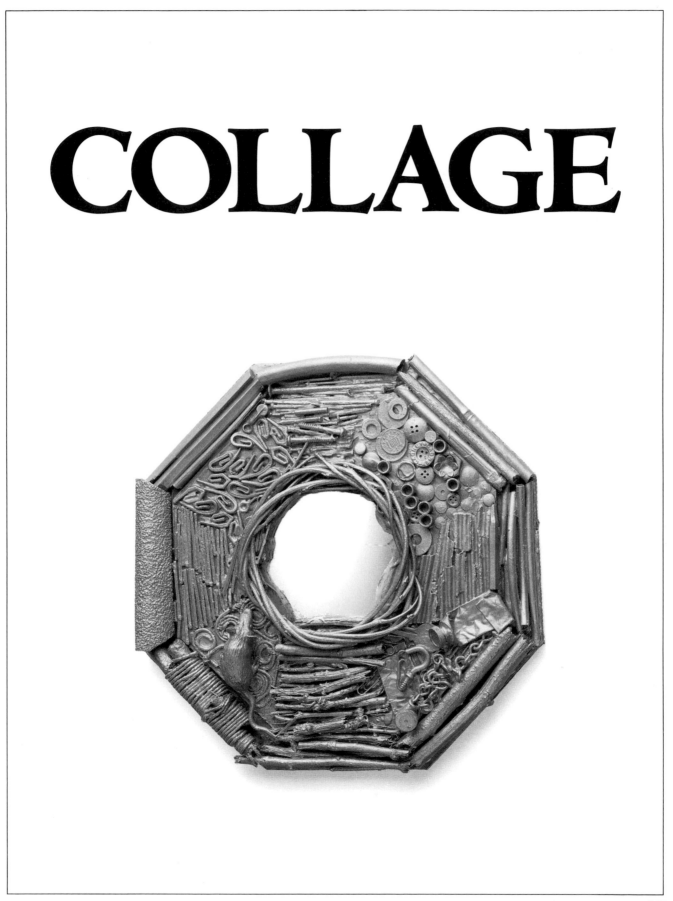

WHAT YOU NEED

Collages are pictures made by pasting down scraps of paper and other odds and ends. You will need scissors, glue, paper, and cardboard, and all the bits of junk you can lay your hands on.

Paper

Paper and cardboard are ideal for making collages. Try to build up a collection that includes some of the following: newspaper, magazines, tissue and crêpe paper, wallpaper, construction paper, wrapping paper, candy wrappers, tinfoil, sandpaper, junk mail, envelopes, postcards, tracing paper, smooth and ridged cardboard.

Add texture to paper by scrunching or folding it, or try wrapping it around a pencil to make curls. Or add patterns, by laying the paper over a raised surface and rubbing with a spoon.

Twigs and leaves

Fabric

Stapler

Hole punch

Fabric

Collages made from fabric are fascinating to touch as well as to look at. Collect scraps of cotton, wool, silk, leather, burlap, lace, and net, as well as ribbons and sequins. Fur fabric is especially fun to work with and can be bought quite cheaply in small quantities.

Bits and Pieces

Start a junk box, and save the following: egg cartons, string, straws, stamps, buttons, corks, beads, small toys, Styrofoam, bubblewrap, screws, washers, nails, nuts and bolts, bottle tops, leaves, shells, twigs, and dried pasta.

Tools of the Trade

In addition to scissors, you may need to use an art knife — these are sharp, so ask an adult to help.

Use safe, simple glues, such as white glue or glue sticks. Tape and a stapler are also useful.

Although collage is about gluing, you can add extra color with paint and glitter.

Finally, you will also need a ruler and pencils.

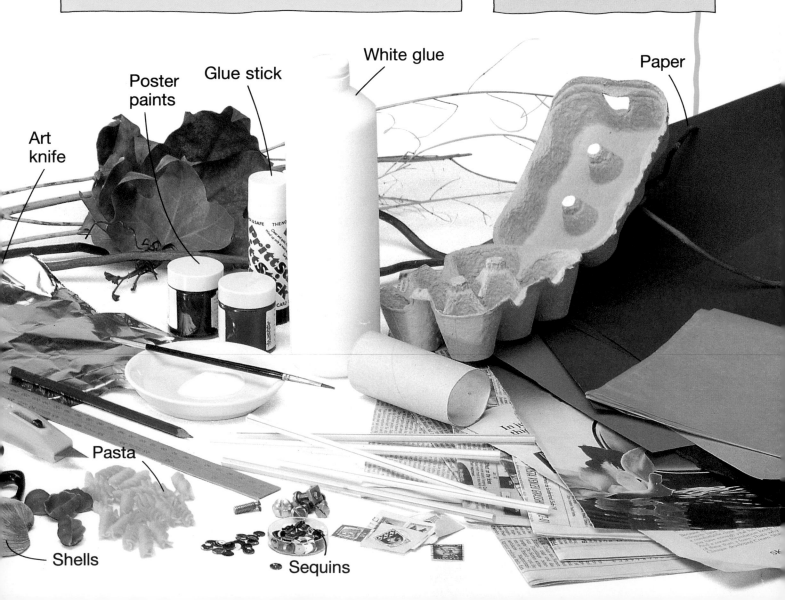

White glue

Glue stick

Poster paints

Paper

Art knife

Pasta

Shells

Sequins

PAPER PATTERNS

Paper is cheap, colorful, and very easy to cut and paste — which makes it perfect for collage. Save old magazines and newspapers, and look out for other types of paper and cardboard *(see page 46).*

Before you start to make pictures from paper, try arranging scraps in abstract patterns as shown here. Making patterns will help you to learn about color, shading, and texture — this will be helpful not only when making collages from paper, but also when you are using fabric and other bits and pieces.

Try combining cut and torn shapes in your pattern using black and white for bold contrast.

Cut dark-colored paper into shapes with scissors or an art knife. Glue them in a pattern onto a sheet of white paper.

In contrast to the clean, sharp lines of the cut paper, a similar pattern made from torn paper has a much softer feel.

For a more subtle contrast, try using the many different *tones* (or shades) of gray that lie between black and white.

48

Experiment with color. Try soft pastel shades (below), or bright, cheerful colors. Which ones clash? Which ones work well together?

Red, orange, and yellow are warm colors. They can appear even warmer when a cool color is placed next to them, as here.

Blue, green, and purple are cool colors. While warm colors appear to come toward you, cool colors often seem to move away.

Try overlapping pieces of tissue paper to make new colors, or to make the same color richer.

Look for patterns in magazines, wallpaper, and wrapping paper. Cut them out, and use them in collage.

Add texture to your collages, mixing some of the many different types of paper. Add scraps of material and other finds.

49

CUT PAPER

Choose strong, bold-colored paper, and cut it into simple shapes to make striking collages. The one shown here is based on collages by the French artist Henri Matisse — try looking through art books in the library for more ideas.

1 Sketch your ideas for a collage, using some colored pencils or crayons.

2 Collect paper for the collage. Check that the colors you choose go well together.

3 Cut the paper into shapes that match those in your drawing. Do the background first.

4 Cut out all the other shapes. Arrange the shapes on top of the background.

5 Move the shapes around until you like the way they look together. Glue them in place.

TORN PAPER

Pictures made from torn paper have a softer look than those made from cut paper. Tearing produces shapes with a feathery edge — if the paper is colored on one side and white on the back, you will also get a white line around part of the shape.

1

Sketch an outline for your collage, and gather your pieces of paper together.

2

Tear the paper into shapes and glue them in place. Overlap with smaller pieces to add details and highlights.

Make a Mosaic

In ancient Rome, buildings were often decorated with mosaics — pictures made from tiny pieces of glass or stone set into plaster. Try making a mosaic from tiny squares of torn paper, as here.

SCRAP PICTURES

Old magazines are ideal for collage. The paper is glossy, brightly colored, and full of patterns and letters which add interest to your finished picture. The magnificent crowing rooster shown below was made from a mixture of torn and cut paper.

Make some sketches for your collage on scrap paper, using colored pencils. Copy the outline on a piece of cardboard, and use it as a base for the collage.

Collect a pile of old magazines. Look for large areas of color, and tear them out. It doesn't matter if the pages have writing or pictures on them.

Tear or cut the pages into shapes for the collage. To make the rooster's tail feathers, press a round lid on the paper and tear around the curve.

Arrange the pieces on the cardboard. Try to contrast bright, rich colors with darker areas. Overlap pieces of paper as shown, and glue in place.

WORDS AND PICTURES

Most newspapers are printed in black type on white paper. However, because the size and thickness of the type varies enormously, some areas look very dark while others are light. Try using this variety of *tone* to make pictures.

1

Find a picture with lots of contrasting tones, (one which contains light, dark, and medium shades). Draw the outlines on cardboard.

2

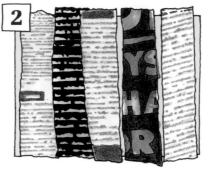

Look through some old newspapers, and tear out pages that have plenty of contrasting light, medium, and dark areas of print.

3

Cut or tear the paper into shapes that match the light and dark areas in your picture. Arrange them in position, and glue them down.

4

You can finish your picture by adding words — try making these by tearing or cutting letters from the paper.

You can also make words by cutting or tearing out the letters themselves from headlines or from other areas of large type.

Combine the letters with pictures cut from newspapers, photo-copies, and magazines — or with drawings you have made yourself.

57

STICK-ONS

Some of the best material for collage is thrown away every day. Save used stamps, stickers, labels from food cans and bottles, seed packets, candy and cookie wrappers, sachets of salt and sugar; and glue them down to make pictures.

1

Draw a mail van and its driver on white cardboard. Draw slightly smaller ones on black paper, and glue on top.

2

Glue the van and driver to colored cardboard or paper. Glue used stamps to the picture, as shown opposite.

3

Use old envelopes as well — postmarks make good wheels and faces. Add features cut from plain black paper.

Cut the labels from cans of fruit, or pictures from color magazines. Use them to make a collage of a bowl of fruit.

Save candy wrappers, and glue them to cardboard to make a picture of a giant candy!

SILHOUETTES

Simple black shapes look dramatic against a light background, or hung up against a window. Draw your design on thin black cardboard or construction paper, and cut out the background with scissors or an art knife. For a stained-glass effect, glue colored tissue paper to the back of the cardboard.

1

2

3

Draw the window frame, witch, and castle on a large sheet of black construction paper. Cut out the background.

Tape wide strips of tissue paper to the back of the frame. Cut out a moon for the light to shine through.

Fold different-sized strips of black paper in half to make bats. Cut them out, and glue to the window.

Try some more designs — how about a prowling panther in a cage? Stained-glass silhouettes are also popular at Christmas — they often show church windows, but you could try making a snowman, a reindeer, or a Santa Claus.

Fabric collages aren't just interesting to look at — they can be fascinating to touch, too. Collect scraps of material, and see what they suggest to you — velvet is soft and luxurious, plastic is smooth, silk is shiny, burlap is rough and coarse. Add more texture with yarn, ribbon, lace, and net.

Sketch a design for your collage, and collect your material. To make this jungle scene, we used fur fabric, leather, curtain samples, scrap paper, and a plastic bag.

Always start with the background. To make a sunset sky, tear orange paper into strips and paste over blue paper.

Cut and paste the jungle in place. The trees in front are wider than those at the back to make them look closer.

The leopard is made from fur fabric, while the frog is made from a green plastic shopping bag! Use more scraps to make the features — sequins are good for highlighting the eyes.

FOOD SHAPES

Dried pasta, beans, lentils, loose tea, and eggshells — many types of dried food can be used in collage. This frog is stuck together with glue in the usual way — but you can also make collages that are good enough to eat! Try making a delicious "collage" on crackers using diced ham, cheese, and tomato — or press candy into the icing on a cake!

1

Draw a frog on cardboard, and cut it out. Collect some dried beans, split peas, lentils, and loose tea.

2

Use a pencil to divide the frog's body into different areas of color. Cover some of these areas with glue.

3

Take a handful of beans or lentils, and press some of them onto the areas you have covered in glue.

4

Contrast the bright orange lentils with the green peas. Use the loose tea to make the black stripes on the frog's body. For an eye, you could glue on a circle of black paper.

5

Use tinfoil to add a glimmer to the eye. You can highlight the frog's "scales" with a little silver paint. Finally, for a shiny wet-look frog, add a coat of varnish.

6

Give your frog a leaf to sit on. This can simply be cut from green cardboard or paper, or made from scraps of green fabric.

SEASCAPE

1

Cut a piece of cardboard, the same size as one side of the box. Glue on a sloping floor.

2

Glue torn colored tissue paper inside the box to make a background scene.

Don't leave beach souvenirs to molder on the windowsill —
turn them into a 3-D collage! You'll need shells, pebbles, and
sand, plus a cardboard box, tissue paper, and thin cardboard.
Old toys with a beach theme can complete the scene.

3

Cut a sand castle from
Styrofoam or thick
cardboard. Cut circles
to make rocks.

4

Glue the rocks and
castle to the floor.
Paint the rocks. Glue
shells to the scene.

5 Brush the floor and castle with glue and sprinkle on sand. Cut out palm tree trunks and leaves from paper.

6 Cut the trunks into segments. Glue each one separately to the back of the box, and tuck in the leaves.

7 Draw gulls' bodies and wings on white cardboard. Cut a slot in the middle of the bodies for the wings, and hang the gulls from the top of the box with thread. Finally, see if you can find some old toys or decorations to add to your scene.

Left: 3-D collages are a great way of displaying your favorite models!

WALL FLOWERS

Once flowers, ferns, and leaves have been thoroughly dried or pressed, they should keep forever. Use them simply to make pictures or cards — or combine them with fake flowers to make a window box bursting with color, like the one overleaf. Never pick wild flowers — they could be very rare.

1

2

3

Pressed Flowers

Press petals, leaves, or ferns in a flower press, or between the pages of a heavy book. Leave them to dry for about a month. The flowers can then be glued into a picture with white glue.

Tissue Flowers

1. Make a simple template from cardboard. Use it to cut about ten flowers from tissue paper — use more than one color if you like.

2. Staple the flowers together in the center.

3. Fold up each petal in turn, as shown.

69

Window box

This midsummer window box can be made to bloom even in the depths of winter — all you need is some colorful paper and cardboard. If you like, you can include pressed flowers and leaves, or silk roses like the ones shown in the picture.

1

Cut a window frame from cardboard or paper. Cut a second frame, with slightly thinner bars, and glue it over the first one.

2

Cut a window box from brown paper. Cut out some "S" shapes, and glue the tips to the window box as shown.

3

Glue all your fake or real flowers to the window box. Fill in the gaps with extra leaves cut from colored cardboard.

JUNK MIRROR

Everything from screws and bolts to straws and string can be used in this project. You can also add toys, or figures modeled from clay.

1

Gather up some junk, glue, a small mirror, and corrugated cardboard.

2

Cut two bases, each the same size. Cut a hole from one base for the mirror, and glue the two bases together.

3

Glue the mirror to the center of the cardboard. Divide the frame into sections, and glue different types of junk to each. Twist some thin garden twigs to make the circle in the center.

4

Paint the mirror frame, and seal it with a coat of varnish. Ask an adult to help you attach a picture hook to the back to hang the mirror up.

CRASH!

If an alien intergalactic space cruiser from the year 3000 were to crash unexpectedly through your bedroom wall, it could look something like this...

1

Make a large cone from thin cardboard. Trim the bottom of the cone to make the shape shown.

2

Cut thick cardboard into a starburst. Paint it black, and glue or tape to the cone when dry.

3

Cut window holes in the cone. Cut fins from cardboard, and glue to the top of the cone.

4

Cover the cone and part of the star with foil, so that it looks like a spaceship crashing through a hole.

5

Glue split peas or lentils to the spaceship to look like rivets. Brush the rivets with silver paint.

6

The little star ship commander was made from pipe cleaners, beads, and colored paper!

EGGOSAURUS

The last dinosaurs died out about 65 million years ago. Some had razor-sharp teeth. Others had weird-looking crests or knobbly horns. But only the terrifying *Eggosaurus* was made from packing material, egg cartons, and plastic bubblewrap...

Draw an outline for the *Eggosaurus* on cardboard, and cut it out. Use it to cut the same shape from bubblewrap, and glue this to the cardboard.

Cut up an egg carton, and glue the cups to the body. You can add extra scaly texture with dried peas or beans, seeds, bottle tops, shells, or net.

Color the *Eggosaurus* with thick poster paint. Cut some red ribbon or paper into a tongue, and glue to the mouth.

Stand the Eggosaurus *among trees with modeling-clay trunks and leaves made from green paper.*

MEMORY BOARD

Vacations, birthdays, or a special day out can all be recorded forever in a collage. All you need to do is to save any scraps or souvenirs and glue them onto a board made from cardboard, cork, or Styrofoam. Hang the board on your wall — every time you look at it, the happy memories will start flooding back!

1

For a Christmas souvenir, cut a piece of thick cardboard into a Christmas tree shape. Paint one side green.

2

Arrange the souvenirs on the board. When you like the way they look together, glue, pin, or staple them in place.

From a dream vacation to a walk in the park, you can use your souvenirs to make a 3-D bulletin board...

COLLAGE CARDS

Homemade cards are a million times nicer than anything you can buy in a store — ask any mom or dad! A selection of collage ideas from the previous pages of this book was used to make the cards shown below. In addition to looking wonderful, they're all incredibly quick and easy to do.

Cut or tear paper into strips, and paste them to make a simple landscape. Use fur fabric or cotton to make the sheep in the foreground.

A hole punch can be a very useful tool in collage. How else could you make a hundred snowflakes in under a minute?

Four airplane-shaped buttons, white pipe cleaners, and a cloud cut from white Styrofoam were used to make this card.

81

MORE IDEAS

By now, you have probably realized that anything that stays still long enough can be turned into a collage. Here are a few ideas you may not have thought of...

Make strange-looking people or animals by cutting up different photos, postcards, or pictures and gluing them together. This is called photomontage...

Paste photos or pictures onto lampshades, wastepaper baskets, boxes, etc. Or glue dried pasta, candy, or cookies to jar lids. Finish them with a coat of varnish...

Collect everything you can about a friend's favorite subject (a sport, movie star, hobby, etc.) and make a collage as a special present.

MAKING KITES

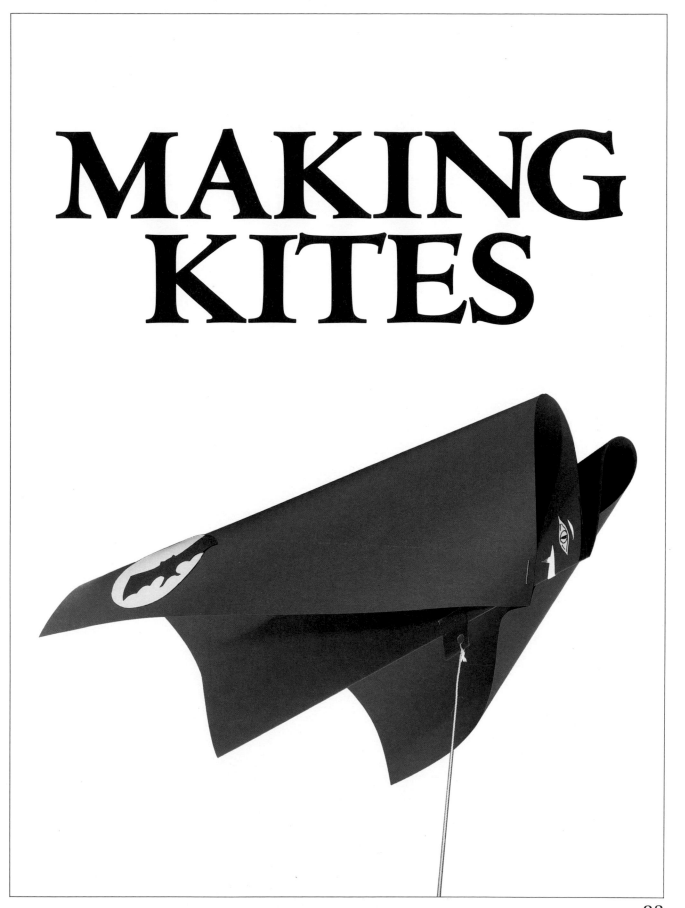

WHAT YOU NEED

To build most of the kites in this book, you will need to buy equipment from a specialist kite or hobby store. You will also need some simple household equipment and a generous working area — kite building takes up a lot of room.

Frame Materials

The *spars* or sticks that make the frame of a kite can be made from a variety of materials.

Bamboo is a traditional material and is still useful for smaller kites.

Wooden sticks can be bought in model and kite shops, as well as hardware stores.

Plastic rods are strong, light, and easily bent. Bigger sizes come in the form of hollow tubes, which reduce the weight.

More expensive, but strongest and lightest sticks of all, are those made from *carbon fiber*.

Center joint

Ripstop nylon

Handle

Swivel clip

Bridle ring

Sail Materials

The sail of a kite can be made from anything that is light and won't tear easily. Light-wind kites can even be made from *paper*. *Plastic* sheeting is probably the best choice for beginners — it is strong, waterproof, and can be repaired with tape. *Coated ripstop nylon* needs to be sewn rather than taped, but it is the first choice of the experienced kite builder.

Lines and Rings

String comes in many different weights, from thin thread for light kites to super-strong, tough enough to lift you off the ground! For your first kites, buy medium-strength string and a simple plastic handle. Later, you may prefer to use string mounted on a reel. Buy aluminum bridle rings, or use curtain rings. A swivel clip lets you add a spinning tail.

Brown paper

Plastic rod

Carbon rod

Hardwood rod

Tools

White craft glue can be used to glue all kite parts. Use tape when you can — invisible, waterproof, and double-sided tape are all useful.

You will also need the following: a craft knife, scissors, a protractor, ruler, a small hacksaw, sandpaper, a compass, a hole punch, and a needle and thread. To make the Hexafringe *(page 115)*, you will need a drill and an adult's help.

Polyester thread

Ready-made tail

85

PARTS OF A KITE

Although the kites in this book all have different designs, the basic parts share the same name. These parts are shown in the diagrams below. On the following pages, you will find everything you need to know about putting the parts together.

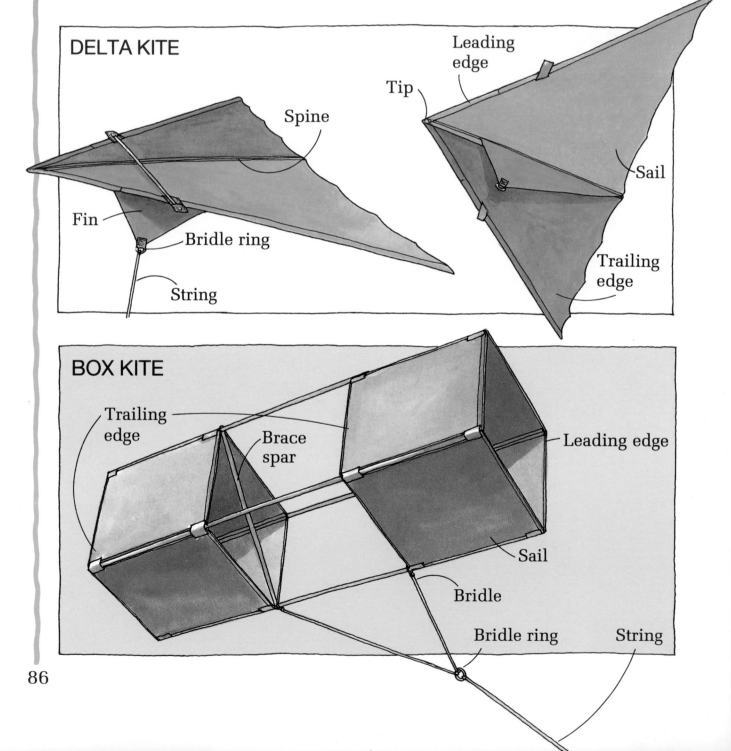

DELTA KITE

Spine

Leading edge

Tip

Sail

Fin

Bridle ring

Trailing edge

String

BOX KITE

Trailing edge

Brace spar

Leading edge

Sail

Bridle

Bridle ring

String

MAKING KITES

Making kites isn't difficult. Follow the instructions carefully, and check your measurements at every stage. If you do, your kites should fly just as well as the ones that we built while making this book!

Making the Frame

To make the spars, cut the dowel, plastic, or carbon rods into lengths with a small hacksaw. Try to keep the sawing even and gradual — if you try to force the spars, they may snap. Use fine sandpaper to smooth the edges of the spar ends.

Joints

To join the spars, you can use strong twine, tape, or glue. For kites with angled sails (for example, the Superstunter *on page 110*), you will need to buy a metal or plastic bent center joint from a kite store. Plastic joints are rigid, but metal joints can be bent to fit the angle of your kite.

Joining Sails

To join plastic, paper, or cardboard, you can use tape. Overlap materials wherever possible, and tape both sides for extra strength. If you are using ripstop nylon, you should sew the pieces with a needle and thread. Overlap the edges by at least half an inch, and try to make the stitches small and neat. For extra strength, stitch two parallel lines, $\frac{1}{4}$ inch apart.

Making Pockets

The spars are kept in place by pockets at the tip, base, and top ends. They are quite simple to make.

Taping Pockets:
Cut a triangle out of strong plastic to match the corner of the sail of the kite.

Use a strip of tape to attach the triangle to the corner of the sail to make a pocket.

Fold down the tip of the pocket to make a straight edge. Tape in place securely.

Sewing Pockets:

Cut a strip from nylon, $3\frac{1}{2}$ x 1 inch. Fold in half and sew as shown. Lay the pocket over the corner of the sail, so that it overlaps the corner. Sew it to the sail — the x-shaped stitching will add extra strength.

Bridle Ring Pocket:

The Delta kite *on page 112* uses a bridle ring pocket. To make it, just follow the stages shown here.

Below: The corner pockets and bridle ring pocket are sewn to ripstop nylon sails, using strong polyester thread.

Attaching Strings

When making kites, you will need to use two main strings. The *bridle* is tied to the kite at one end (using a bowline knot) and to a *bridle ring* at the other end (using a lark's head knot). The *string* is then tied to the bridle ring with a bowline knot. These two knots are shown below.

Lark's Head Knot

Bowline Knot

TAILS

Tails are not only colorful and attractive. They have a practical use, too. They make a kite more stable in the air and are essential for many designs, such as the Diamond Two-stick on page 102, and other kites with flat sails.

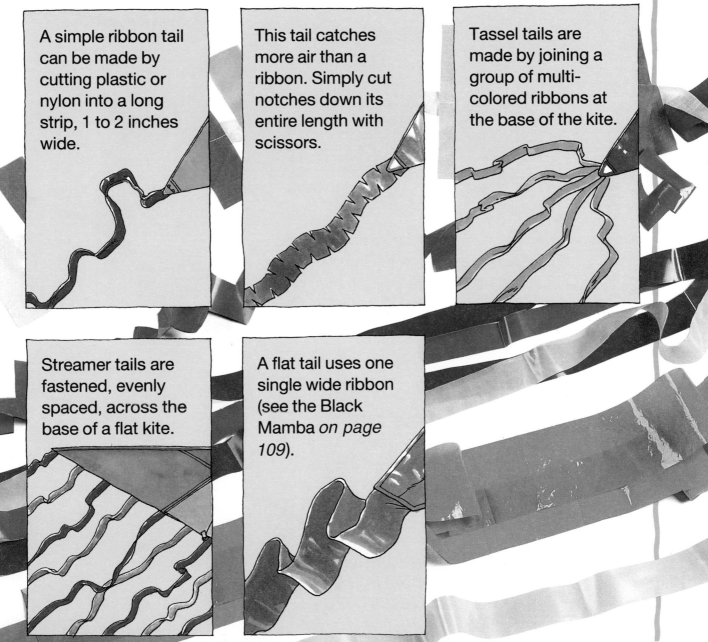

A simple ribbon tail can be made by cutting plastic or nylon into a long strip, 1 to 2 inches wide.

This tail catches more air than a ribbon. Simply cut notches down its entire length with scissors.

Tassel tails are made by joining a group of multi-colored ribbons at the base of the kite.

Streamer tails are fastened, evenly spaced, across the base of a flat kite.

A flat tail uses one single wide ribbon (see the Black Mamba *on page 109*).

DECORATIONS

For added interest, try making some of the decorations shown here. They add color and stability to the kite, and look spectacular in the air.

Spinning Helix

This kite looks hypnotically attractive as it spins round and round in the wind.

1 Using a plate as a guide, cut a large circle out of light cardboard or shiny Melinex.

2 Mark a point $\frac{3}{4}$ to $1\frac{1}{4}$ inches from the edge. Make a slanted cut to form the end of the tail.

$\frac{3}{4}$–$1\frac{1}{4}$ in.

3 Keep cutting in a spiral until you reach the center. Keep the lines $\frac{3}{4}$ to $1\frac{1}{4}$ inches apart.

4 Attach the helix to the base of your kite, using a swivel clip (available from a kite shop).

Wind sock

This can be made from nylon, plastic, or (as here) from shiny plastic wrapping paper.

Cut out a rectangle of the paper, making the sides 16 x 12$\frac{1}{2}$ in. Cut as shown, so that the trailing edge measures 11$\frac{1}{2}$ in. across. Roll up into a tube, and tape

along the inside. Cut four pieces of string into 15-in. lengths, and cut a 13-in. piece of tape. Position the ends of the string along the sticky side, spacing the pieces

equally as shown above. Roll the wider end of the wind sock carefully along the tape. Tie the loose ends of string together, and tie to the base of the kite.

Cut the end of the wind sock into a pointed pattern. If you like, cut diamonds out of the sides, as shown.

93

Tailspinner

This tailspinner spins around in the wind, sending its ribbons flying through the air.

Making the Tailspinner

1 — 36 in. — / 5 in.

Cut eight triangles out of plastic or nylon. Make each triangle about 5 inches on the short end. Cut a band 1 yard in length from ripstop nylon. Sew on the triangles, overlapping each one by $\frac{1}{2}$ inch at the top.

2

Cut two tail disks out of plastic or nylon. Use a compass to make sure they measure $1\frac{1}{4}$ inches across. Glue the tips of the triangles under the tips of one of the circles, then glue the second circle underneath the triangle tips.

94

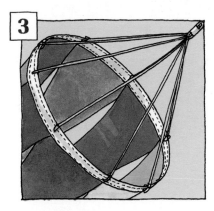

3

Cut eight pieces of kite string, each 10 inches long. Tape them to the band and tie the other ends to a swivel clip.

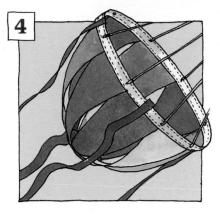

4

Tie or sew on four streamers made from bright pieces of plastic. These whirl around in a spiral.

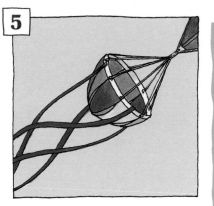

5

Attach the swivel clip to the base of the kite. Or, if you prefer, clip the tailspinner halfway up the kite string.

Climbing the line

When your kite is flying in the sky, what else can you do?
Try slotting this little spinner up the line, and letting go. . .

Cut a 4-inch-diameter disk from stiff cardboard. Make a hole (about $\frac{1}{8}$ inch wide) through the center.

Use a compass to draw four $1\frac{1}{3}$ inch circles. Cut out half the circles, and bend up as shown. Cut the line A to B.

Cut a $2\frac{1}{3}$-inch length of plastic straw, and cut a lengthwise slit in it. Glue in the center of the disk at right angles, so that both cuts line up.

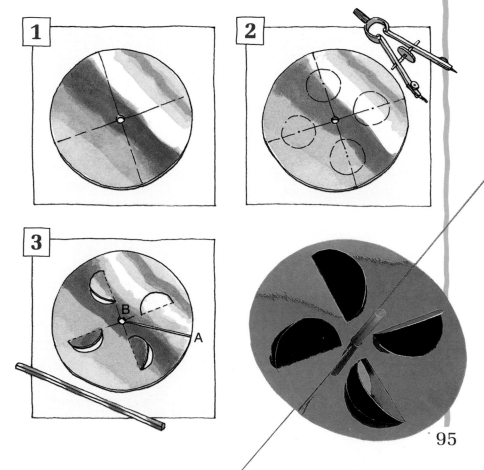

FLIGHT TESTING

The test flight is the moment of truth — have you built the kite well? Will it fly, or will it crash? Will it even get off the ground? Hopefully, it will soar like a bird — but you may need to adjust the balance first. Always choose open land to fly in, and don't try to fly the kite in very strong winds or when the air is still.

WIND DIRECTION

Launching is easier with two people. Unwind 20-30 feet of string and pull it taut. Make sure that your helper is facing into the wind. He or she should raise the kite into the air, with the kite facing the wind. Pull firmly on the string — the kite should soar up. If it doesn't, try walking backward or give a few sharp tugs on the kite string.

Flight Safety

* Keep away from electricity wires, trees, and houses.

* Don't fly kites near airfields, or at heights which may get in the way of aircraft.

* Use leather gloves if it is very windy. The string can burn the hands if it unwinds suddenly.

* Don't fly in stormy weather. Lightning could strike the kite and kill you.

* Don't launch the kite if people or animals are walking past.

Adjusting the Balance

A kite that flies perfectly one day may fly badly the next time you take it out — this may be due to a change in wind conditions. Try moving the bridle ring.

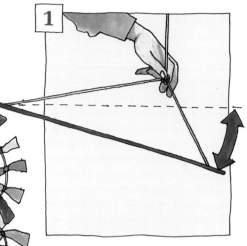

1

Before flight, hold the kite by the bridle ring. Adjust the ring so that the kite hangs at 20-30° into the wind.

2

Moving the bridle forward makes the kite fly higher, at a flat angle to the wind. This is good for smooth winds.

3

Moving the bridle back makes the kite fly at a steeper angle. Use in medium to gusty wind conditions.

1

2

3

Trouble Shooting

Kite fails to rise: not enough wind, bridle too short, or tail too long.

Kite flies, then crashes: bridle may need to be shortened.

Kite spins or wobbles: add more tail.

Landing your kite

To land your kite, wind in the string on your reel. If the wind is quite strong, try pulling the string in hand over hand until the kite comes down.

DRACULA'S CLOAK

All kinds of simple kites can be made out of paper. Dracula's Cloak can be made out of plain white paper, but it looks much more sinister in purple or black. It flies well in a gentle breeze.

Instead of painting your kite, try cutting shapes out of colored paper and gluing them on the surface with white paste.

1

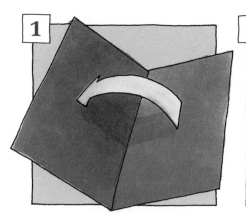

Fold a $11\frac{1}{2}$ x $16\frac{1}{2}$-inch sheet of typing-weight paper carefully across the middle as shown above.

2

$1\frac{1}{3}$ in.

Pull one side of the sheet around in a curve. Staple it against the center fold, $1\frac{1}{3}$ inches from the tip.

3

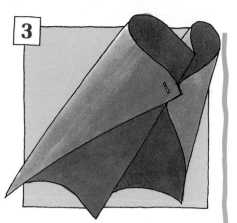

Repeat on the other side. Make sure the corners slightly overlap the center fold, as shown above.

4

$3\frac{1}{2}$ in.

The Dracula's Cloak kite doesn't need a bridle ring. Just cut a square piece of thick tape and press it on the center

5

fold, $3\frac{1}{2}$ inches from the tip. Make a hole in the tape as shown in the picture with a hole punch or a pair of scissors.

Use lightweight thread to fly the Cloak. It will rise in the lightest breeze and hover menacingly above you!

Dracula's Cloak takes on a bloodthirsty look if you paint some talons, fangs, and a leering face on it. Use felt-tip pens on white paper, and poster paints on colored paper.

6

TWIN-FIN SKYSLED

Another good flyer in light winds, this kite can be made out of paper or plastic. The one shown here is a good pocket-sized kite, but it could also be made on a larger scale.

Colored tape was used to decorate this Twin-Fin. You could also use bright poster paint.

1

Mark a center line down the middle of a piece of paper $11\frac{1}{2}$ x $16\frac{1}{2}$ inches. Do not fold the sheet, as this will spoil flight performance.

2

Fold both ends in to the center line. Cut the sides in the triangle pattern shown — the tips should be $2\frac{3}{4}$ inches from the end of the kite.

3

Cut out the two twin-fin stabilizers. Heavy paper fins can be folded up. Plastic ones will flop until they are blown by the wind.

4

Strengthen the corners to take the strain of the bridle. It is simplest to use strong tape and to make the holes with a hole punch.

5

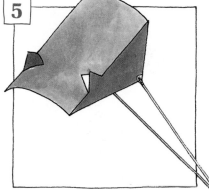

Tie on a long bridle, two to three times the length of the kite. Start with 27 inches, and adjust if necessary.

Use Melinex or shiny wrapping paper to make a kite which dazzles like an alien spacecraft in the sky!

DIAMOND TWO-STICK

The Diamond Two-stick is a classic kite design. The one shown here has two bridle rings — use the top ring in light winds, the bottom one for stronger conditions. Add a longer tail if the kite wobbles in flight.

1

Cut two triangles out of plastic sheeting or rip-stop nylon. Make them the same size, and allow an extra $\frac{3}{8}$-inch overlap on the spine edge.

3

Sew or tape the two sails together. Join them along their longest sides, as shown above. Sew or tape on the fin, positioning it $3\frac{1}{2}$ inches from the tip of the kite.

2

Cut out a fin, allowing $\frac{3}{8}$-inch overlap. Cover the corner with tape, punch two holes, and slip on two split rings.

4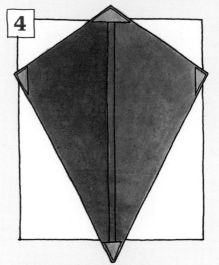

Tape or sew triangular pockets to the tip, base, and sail ends. They need to be very strong, so use thicker material than the sail fabric.

5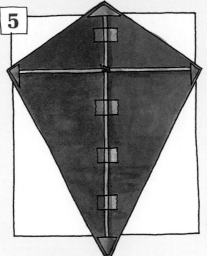

Cut two pieces of dowel ($\frac{1}{4}$-inch diameter) to fit the kite. Slide in place and tie them where they cross. Tape the spine stick to the sail, or sew cotton tape to the sail and tie to the spars.

6

Cut four plastic tails, each measuring 2 inches wide x 6 feet long. Attach two of them to the base of the kite with a safety pin. Add the other two tails if the kite isn't a stable flyer. Attach the kite string to the top or bottom bridle ring, depending on wind conditions.

THE RINGWING

This Ringwing was made out of thin cardboard and $\frac{1}{4}$-inch diameter carbon fiber rod. It flies well, but needs a strong wind for a good liftoff.

1 Cut a 36-inch-long piece of dowel or carbon fiber rod. Smooth the ends with sandpaper.

2 Cut two pieces of thin cardboard, each 10 x 27 inches. Press double-sided tape on one end of each sheet.

10 in.

27 in.

3 Fold the ends around to form circular sails. Press firmly over the taped edge to make sure it is secure.

4 Use white glue to attach each sail to the spar, and tape them in place. Try to make sure the sails are perfectly straight.

For a vertical takeoff, make the spar 4 inches longer behind the rear wing. Anchor it into the ground at takeoff, and pull the string firmly. If the wind is right, the kite should soar into the air like a jump jet.

5

Tie the bridle to the points shown. Use a strong kite string, and wear gloves to protect your hands — the Ringwing can pull hard, and the string can burn.

FRONT SAIL

REAR SAIL

Adjust the bridle ring so that the Ringwing hangs at an angle of 20 to 30°.

105

BOX KITE

The sails of this box kite are made from acoustic tiles. They can be bought in hardware stores, and come in standard sizes — usually 12 inches square. The frame is made from $\frac{1}{4}$-inch diameter wooden dowel.

1

Lay four tiles in a straight line on a flat surface. Make sure that the angled edges are face down. Tape the tiles together at the edges. Then fold them into a box shape, and tape together on the inside, as shown below.

2

Make another sail the same way, making sure that the edges are evenly taped.

3

Cut the dowels into four spars, each 36 inches long. Glue to the sails with white glue, and hold in place with tape. The spars should fit into the angled corners of the cubes as shown.

4

To keep the kite rigid, you will need to cut two $12\frac{1}{2}$-inch vertical spars out of the dowel rod. Notch, glue, and tie them in position as shown.

5

Tie a bridle on as shown above. Paint the kite — you can use brushes, or spray paint (but not the type made for painting cars!)

107

THE BLACK MAMBA

The sight of the Mamba slithering across the sky is enough to send a shiver down the strongest spine — yet it's little more than a cleverly sliced plastic garbage bag.

1 Cut three lengths of $\frac{1}{8}$-inch diameter plastic rod to make a T-shape, as shown in the diagram. Fasten the three rods together with tape.

2 Cut open a black plastic garbage bag, and lay the frame on top. Tape the spine and base. Trim the plastic, leaving $\frac{3}{4}$ inch at the top and bottom.

3 Bend down the top rod so that the ends are $4\frac{1}{4}$ inches below the tip. Tape the plastic securely, and trim the sides as shown.

$4\frac{1}{4}$ in.

Cut sinister features from colored paper or plastic and glue them on the Mamba's face.

4

Tape the edges — this adds strength to the kite and prevents it from ripping in strong winds, or when it is coming in to land.

5

Cut the rest of the bag into 6-inch-wide strips. Tape them together to make a long tail, and cut the end into a point. Tape the flat edge to the base of the kite. Make two holes as shown, and tie on a bridle — adjust it if you need to improve the Mamba's flight.

109

THE SUPERSTUNTER

Take command of the air with this twin-line kite! The two lines let you climb, dive, spin, and soar, but be warned — the Superstunter is a nervous flyer, and the slightest mistake will send it hurtling to the ground.

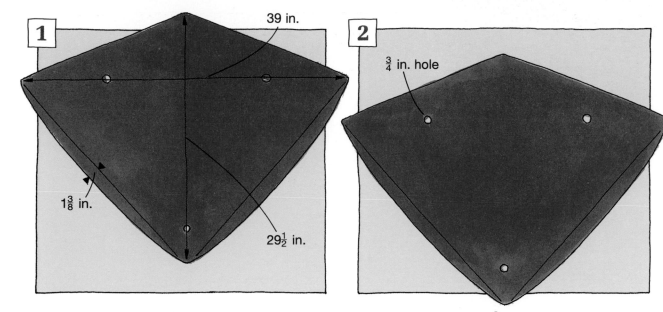

1 39 in.

$1\frac{3}{8}$ in.

$29\frac{1}{2}$ in.

2 $\frac{3}{4}$ in. hole

Draw this sail plan on a large sheet of paper to the sizes shown. Cut out, and pin to a sheet of plastic. Cut out the plastic sail.

Make three holes, $\frac{3}{4}$ inch across, for the bridle. Then tape a plastic pocket (buy these from a kite store, or make your own) into each corner.

3

4

6 in.

5

Cut four pieces of $\frac{1}{4}$-inch dowel to fit the sail. Put into a metal joint, and slip the ends into the pockets.

To make the angled wing, keep one wing flat on your work surface and bend up the other wing.

Two bridles are used for this kite. Tie them to the spars through the holes, as shown above.

6

Tie on the bridle rings, and tie to two separate kite strings. Make tails by cutting old plastic bags into streamers and taping them to the base of the kite.

111

DELTA STAR

Use adhesive shapes as a quick way of decorating your Delta.

This classic design flies in light winds and is very stable. It can be made from plastic and tape or sewn in ripstop nylon like the one shown here. Add long pennants and streamers for extra interest.

1

$\frac{3}{4}$ in.

$31\frac{1}{2}$ in.

$31\frac{1}{2}$ in.

$\frac{3}{4}$ in.

$11\frac{1}{2}$ in.

$21\frac{1}{4}$ in.

$13\frac{3}{4}$ in.

Draw two right-angled triangles measuring $31\frac{1}{2}$ inches on the short sides. Allow an extra

$\frac{3}{4}$ inch on the inside and leading edges, and cut out. Draw a smaller triangle measuring $11\frac{1}{2}$ x

$13\frac{3}{4}$ x $21\frac{1}{4}$ inches, for the stabilizer fin. Allow an extra $\frac{3}{4}$ inch on the longest side, and cut out.

2

Fold the leading edges over, and sew to make a pocket for the wing spars.

3

Sew the spine edges together with a double seam casing to make a casing for the spine spar.

4

Attach the fin to the spine as shown by sewing down the side of

the spine spar casing. Sew a bridle ring pocket to the fin *(see page 89)*.

113

5

6

Make two pockets for the cross-brace spar. Sew the pockets to the leading edges, as shown on page 88. Make sure that the pockets are positioned 20 inches from the tip of the kite.

Make spars for the spine and leading edges from $\frac{1}{4}$-inch dowel cut into 8-inch lengths.

7

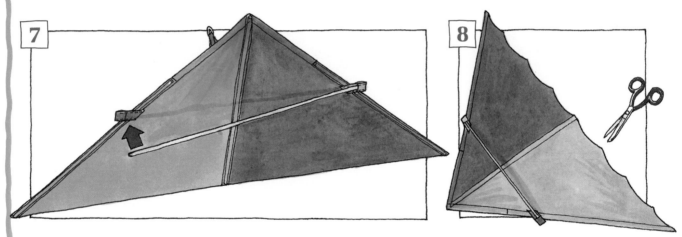

8

Cut another piece of $\frac{1}{4}$-inch dowel $31\frac{1}{2}$ inches long. This is the cross-brace spar. Slip the ends of the spar into the two pockets you have attached to the leading edges of the kite.

If you like, cut a scalloped edge along the base of the Delta, as shown above.

Decorate the Delta with adhesive stars, and attach tails to the base. You could also add a tailspinner *(page 94)*, or even tie on a banner with a message!

9

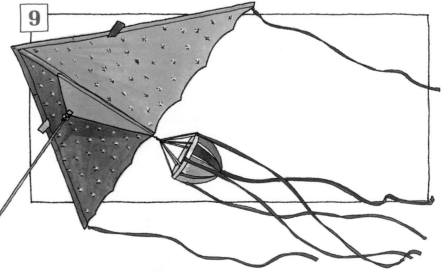

HEXAFRINGE

The design for this six-sided kite comes from Greece, a land of sea and sunshine. On a sunny day, the kite's many-colored fringe and long tail make it one of the prettiest you are likely to see. To make it, you will need to do some drilling — ask an adult to help you.

1

Draw the pattern shown above on a large sheet of newspaper. Use a protractor to make each angle measure 60°.

Cut $\frac{1}{4}$-inch-square wooden sticks into three $31\frac{1}{2}$-inch lengths. Smooth the ends with sandpaper. Using a very small drill bit, make a hole $\frac{1}{8}$ inch from the end of each stick.

Tape the sticks to the pattern, one on top of the other. Make sure that the holes are on the sides. Then firmly tie the sticks in the middle with twine. Remove the pattern.

2

3

Drill four more holes, A, B, C, and D, 2 inches from the end of the spars. These are for the bridles. Finally, drill holes E and F, $\frac{3}{8}$ inch from the ends. These are for the tail. Screw eyehooks into all these six holes.

Tape the spars firmly to a large sheet of brown wrapping paper with the eyehooks pointing down. Cut the paper into a hexagonal sail, as shown — the spars must be 2 inches longer than the sail.

Use poster paint to decorate the sail, or glue shapes cut from colored paper.

Thread a long length of fishing line or strong thread through the side holes at the end of the spars, and tie firmly. This line supports the fringe of the kite.

7

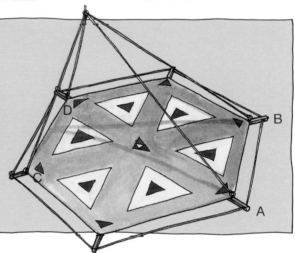

Cut four pieces of kite string for the bridle. Tie one end of a piece of string to each eyehook (marked A, B, C, and D). Then tie the free ends to a bridle ring. You will need to adjust the length of each bridle line, so that when the kite is held by the bridle ring, the four lines meet at a point directly above and in the middle of points C and D (see the diagram above).

Cut two more pieces of string, and tie them to the eyehooks E and F. Tie them together so that the lines run parallel to the edges of the kite.

8

Make a tail from pieces of colored plastic — shopping bags are ideal. Try 3 yards to begin with — you may need to add more later.

9

10

Make a fringe out of plastic or paper. Cut six strips, about 3 inches wide and the same length as the sides of the kite. Fold them over the edge threads, tape in place, and cut a fringe.

The Hexafringe likes a steady breeze best of all. It is a good climber and in a strong wind will rise as fast as you can play out the string.

11

119

MORE IDEAS

Once you feel confident about making kites, you might like to try designing your own. In the meantime, here are a few more ideas for you to consider....

All you need is a thin plastic raincoat (the kind that folds into a pocket), and two wooden spars!

Based on ancient Chinese designs, this flying fish is little more than a decorated wind sock.

Tie balloons to the ends of poles, and use stunt kites to try to burst them. It's harder than you might think.

This tiny kite is only 1 inch across, but it can fly in front of a mini fan. Use very light sail material.

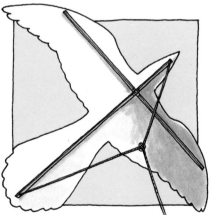

Kites in the shape of birds are fun. A prehistoric version could be made in the shape of a pterosaur.

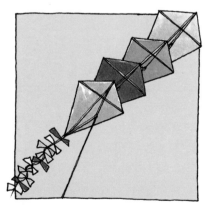

Flying a stack of matching kites is a popular sport. The stable Delta kite is well suited to stacking.

120

PAPIER MÂCHÉ

WHAT YOU NEED

Shown below are the main things you will need to make the models in this book. Before you start on a project, read through the step-by-step instructions to make sure that you have any extra items that are not listed here.

Paper

Although you can use many different types of paper to make papier-mâché (including tissue paper and any paper that is thin and absorbent), newspaper is by far the easiest (and the cheapest) to use.

Glue and Tape

White glue is useful for sticking the papier-mâché parts together. (It can also be used instead of varnish for a final coat.) Use masking tape to hold the parts in place until the glue dries.

Mineral spirits (for cleaning brushes after varnishing)

White latex paint

Gouache paint

Masking tape

Wallpaper Paste

Most wallpaper pastes contain fungicide — this is poisonous, so keep it away from small children, and don't get it in your eyes, nose, or mouth! You can also make a homemade paste out of flour and water. Heat 6 cups of water and 3 cups of flour in a pan. Keep stirring, until it looks like thick cream. Leave to cool.

SAFETY TIP:
You will need to use a sharp knife to make some of the things in this book. Be sure that you always ask an adult to help you.

Junk

Keep a collection of junk, such as cardboard tubes, cereal boxes, bottles, string, wire, foil, and corrugated paper. For some of the models, you will also need some modeling clay, and a bag of balloons.

Paints and Varnish

You will need white latex, gouache, or poster paints, and some varnish (see page 126). You will also need a small brush for decorating, a medium-sized paintbrush, and a thin brush for fine details.

Petroleum jelly

Wallpaper paste

Decorating brush

Varnish

Fine brushes

Waterproof ink

Poster paint

123

BASIC TECHNIQUES

Most of the models in the book are made by pasting strips of paper over a *mold* (such as a bowl), or a *framework* (such as a cardboard box). You can also make pulp, which is modeled just like clay.

Using Molds

Always grease your molds with lots of petroleum jelly before you put on the papier- mâché. This makes it much easier to remove the mold later on.

Using Frameworks

Bottles, tubes, boxes, and other pieces of junk can be used as frameworks for papier-mâché. Unlike molds, these are not removed when the paper is dry.

Paper Strips

Always tear the paper rather than cutting it — this gives a smoother finish. It's a good idea to work with two piles of different-colored paper, and to change color when you start a new layer — this helps you to see where one layer ends and the new one starts.

Pasting Strips

Make the paste, following the directions on the package. Cover each strip with paste, and smooth over the mold or framework. Overlap them slightly, until the object is completely covered. Repeat for all other layers.

Drying Out

When you've put on all the layers, leave the papier-mâché to dry out completely in a warm, dry place. As a rough guide, a bowl made from 7 layers of papier-mâché will take two to three days to dry out.

Below: These models were all made by pressing pulp into cooking molds.

Making Pulp

Take 8 large sheets of newspaper, and tear into tiny squares. Cover with hot water, and leave to soak for 24 hours. Ask an adult helper to boil the paper and water for 20 minutes. Leave to cool. Ask your helper to beat the mixture with an electric hand beater. Pour into a strainer, and press out most of the liquid. Add wallpaper paste until the mixture feels like soft modeling clay.

Using Pulp

Pulp can be modeled with your fingers like clay. It can also be pressed into cooking molds. Leave to dry completely — it will take longer to dry than papier-mâché that has been made from strips.

125

DECORATING IDEAS

Bright poster or gouache paint brings papier-mâché magically to life! Experiment with color — bold primary colors and soft pastels both work well, while gold and silver can make a model look as if it is made of metal. Always give your papier-mâché a coat of white latex before you begin, and finish with at least one coat of varnish.

If you don't feel confident enough to paint a design onto your models, try some of the decorating ideas shown below.

Spattering

Paint a base color over your papier-mâché. Dip an old toothbrush or a nailbrush in a second color. Flick the brush gently with your finger, so that the paint spatters over the surface.

Rag Rolling

Instead of painting your papier-mâché with a brush, try dipping a crumpled rag or a piece of sponge into light-colored paint and then pressing or rolling it lightly over the surface. Repeat with one or more darker colors for a mottled effect that looks rather like stone (see the Greek urn on page 131). This painting technique is useful for covering up a bumpy surface!

Torn Paper

Bowls and plates can look fantastic if you use torn-up colored tissue paper or wrapping paper as a final layer. Scraps of silk can even be glued on in this way. You could also try painting on a base coat in the usual way and decorating with a mosaic made up of tiny squares of paper *(see page 129)*.

Découpage

Paint a base color onto your papier-mâché. Cut out pictures or shapes from magazines, wrapping paper, or plain colored paper, and glue them to the painted surface.

Raised Surfaces

Glue pieces of string, split peas, shapes cut from cardboard, or lumps of pulp onto papier-mâché before painting with white latex.

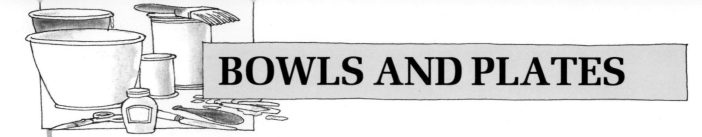

BOWLS AND PLATES

Lots of objects can be used as molds for bowls, plates, and trays. In addition to dishes from the kitchen, you could use a ball or a blown-up balloon. Use at least seven layers of paper — more if you want your bowl or plate to be really thick and strong.

1

Cover the inside of a bowl, wok, or plate with petroleum jelly. Do the same around the rim and the outside edge.

2

Paste on at least 7 layers of paper strips. Leave in a warm place for 2-3 days, or until completely dry.

3

Run a blunt knife between the papier-mâché and the mold and gently ease the papier-mâché off.

4

5

6

Trim the edges with scissors. Paste over the cut edge with 2 layers of small strips and leave to dry.

Paint both sides with latex. When dry, paint on your design, or glue on pieces of colored paper.

Give both sides of the bowl a coat of varnish. This will protect the bowl, but won't make it waterproof.

Below: The two bowls were both molded around a wok, while a china mold was used for the plate on the left. The bowl on the right has a mosaic design, made by gluing tiny squares of paper onto a painted background.

129

Legs and Bases

Glue an empty tape roll under the bowl. If you want, you can glue a circle of cardboard under it. Or make feet from small cones *(page 132)*. Cover with 2 layers of strips.

Making Rims

Coat small strips of paper with paste, and roll up into a thin sausage shape. Wrap it around the outside of the rim, and hold it in place with extra paper strips.

Making Handles

Cut handles from cardboard. Bend back the flaps, and glue to the sides of the bowl. Or make slits with a knife, and glue in the ends of the handles. Paper over with strips.

Rolled-up Roses

Make roses by tearing strips of paper, about 4 x 10 inches. Cover one side with paste, and fold in half. Paste again, and roll around the end of a paintbrush to make a rose. Paste onto the side of the bowl, with leaves cut from cardboard. Paper over the leaves and the seams with 2 layers of strips.

130

The "Greek urn" was rag-rolled (see page 126) and decorated with pictures cut out of a magazine. The yellow bowl has cardboard cone legs. The third bowl was decorated with string, painted blue, and then rubbed over with a rag dipped in gold paint.

PIGGY BANK

Balloons are often used as molds for papier-mâché. Here's a piggy bank to make — just add a yogurt container for a snout, pieces of cardboard for ears and legs, and a pipe cleaner for a tail. To collect your savings, just cut a hole in the bottom — you could use a plastic cap to plug the hole.

1

Blow up a round or an oval balloon, and cover with petroleum jelly. Paste on 5 layers of paper strips, and leave to dry for about 2 days.

2

Cut 2 ears from cardboard. Draw around a small bowl onto cardboard to make 2 circles, and cut out. Cut circles in half, and tape into cones for legs.

3

Burst the balloon with a pin, and pull it out. Paste the ears, legs, and the yogurt container onto the body with white glue. Hold in place with masking tape.

4

Make a hole at the back with a pin. Bend a pipe cleaner into a curly tail, push into the hole, and glue in place. Cover with two layers of strips.

5

Cover the ears, legs, and snout with 2 layers of paper. Leave to dry. Ask an adult to cut a slit in the top with a sharp knife.

Pigs don't have to be pink! Why not decorate with stars, flowers, polka dots, or the owner's name?

6

Paint your piggy bank with a good strong color. When it's finished, use at least one layer of varnish to protect and strengthen it.

MAKING MASKS

All kinds of wonderful masks can be made from papier-mâché. Try gluing on string, yarn, or tinfoil — our tiger has ears and a nose made out of cardboard and whiskers made from bristles taken from an old brush. A gold glitter pen was used to add shimmering highlights to the stripes.

1

Blow up a balloon to your head size. Cover half with petroleum jelly, and paste on 5 layers of paper.

2

Dry for 2 days. Take the mask off, and trim with scissors. Ask an adult to cut out the eyes with a sharp knife.

3

Make the ears and nose from cardboard, and glue them to the head. Tape in place until the glue dries.

4

Paste 2 layers of paper over the ears and across the nose. Pad the sides with rolls of pasted paper.

5

When dry, paint both sides with latex. Color with poster paint, and finish with two coats of clear varnish.

6

Use a thick needle to make a hole on each side. Thread with elastic, and adjust to fit the size of your head.

Try making scary masks for Halloween, crazy carnival masks, or funny faces for plays and disguises.

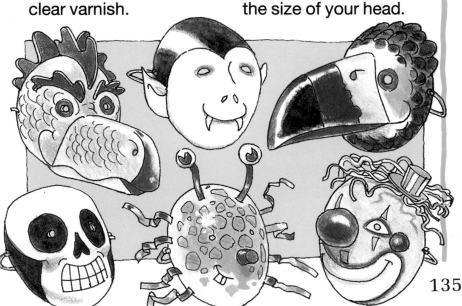

135

FLYING MACHINES

Make hot-air balloons and airships from different-shaped balloons. Paint bright designs on them, add a coat of glossy varnish, and hang from the ceiling with thread.

1 Blow up an oval balloon, and grease with petroleum jelly. Cover with 6 layers of paper strips, and dry.

2 Burst the balloon and pull it out. Cut a large yogurt container in half. Glue the top half to the end of the balloon.

5

3 Cover both container halves with 3 layers of strips, papering over the joint between the balloon and container.

4 Seal the balloon and basket with white latex. Paint brightly and finish with a coat of varnish.

Push a threaded needle down through the balloon, and attach a button. Knot the thread under the button. Pull the button up to the top of the balloon. Attach the basket using a needle and thread.

Airship

Cover a long balloon with paper strips. Glue 2 curved pieces of cardboard together and support with a strip of cardboard in the middle. Cut a propellor, and attach with a pin.

Loop lengths of thread through the gondola, and hang them over the airship. Glue a bent paper clip into the airship to hang it up.

FUN FRUIT

Fill a bowl with fake fruit — or pile it up on top of a carnival hat, as shown on *page 141*. Delicious-looking vegetables can also be made in a very similar way — or how about a hamburger and fries?

Bananas and Watermelons

Make a simple framework by taping curved pieces of cardboard together (it doesn't matter if the edges don't meet exactly). Paper over with 3 layers of strips.

Grapes, Cherries, and Strawberries

Make these from little balls of paper pulp. When the grapes are dry, glue them in a bunch onto a piece of cardboard.

Oranges and Lemons

Crumple up a piece of paper towel. Wrap another piece around the first one, then add a third and fourth. Use masking tape to mold the paper into the shape you need. Cover with 3 layers of pasted strips (it's easiest if you let each layer dry before you add the next). Paint to look as real as possible.

Pineapple

Blow up a small balloon. Cover with 7 layers of strips, and leave to dry. Cut a wide strip of thin cardboard, and cut into pointed leaves with scissors. Glue to the top of the balloon as shown, and paper over the joint. Paint the base color, then the main sections, and finally the detail in each section.

139

FRUIT HAT

This incredible carnival hat may look top heavy — but as it's made from papier-mâché, it's very light and easy to wear.

First, you will need to blow up a balloon until it's the size of your head. Cover with seven layers of paper strips, and leave until completely dry.

1

Cover both sides of a paper plate with 3 layers of pasted strips. Leave to dry.

2

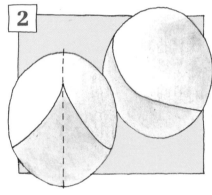

Copy the pattern above onto the covered balloon, and cut away the bottom section.

3

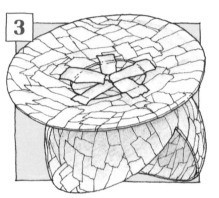

Glue and tape the plate to the hat — this is easier if you cut a hole in the base of the plate.

4

Paper over the joint and the cut edges with small paper strips. When dry, paint and varnish the hat in the usual way.

5

Glue papier-mâché fruit, plastic fruit, or flowers onto the plate. Hook real or papier-mâché earrings (see page 154) onto the hat.

6

HELMET

Silver poster paint and a coat of matte varnish are used to make this helmet look as if it is made of metal.

1

Cover a balloon with 7 layers of strips. When dry, copy the pattern shown here, and cut out with scissors.

2

Make a cone from a large semicircle of cardboard. The cone should fit snugly over the front of the helmet.

3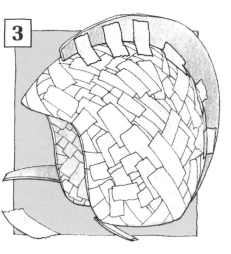

Cut a crest out of cardboard, and tape to the top. Don't worry if there are gaps between the crest and the helmet.

4

Cut a smaller cardboard crescent for the back of the helmet, and tape in position.

5

Cover the cone, crest, and back of the helmet with 3 layers of papier-mâché. Leave to dry.

6

Fold a strip of cardboard in half. Lay a piece of string along the crease, and glue to the cone.

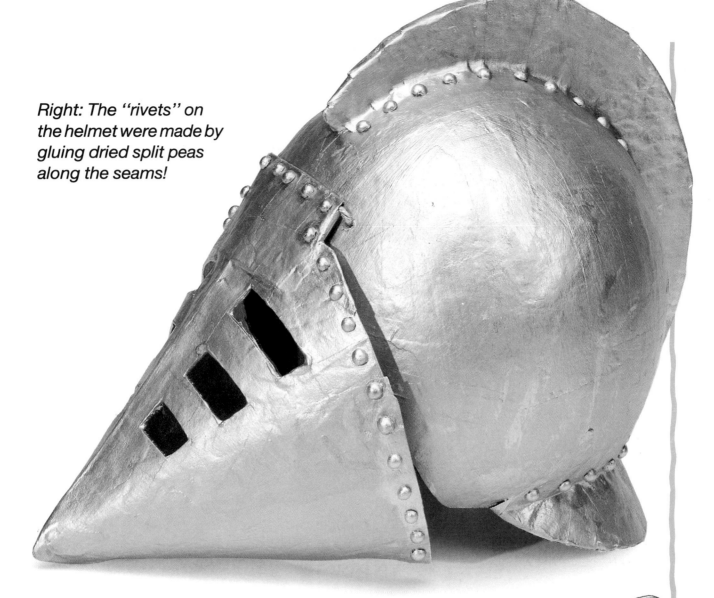

Right: The "rivets" on the helmet were made by gluing dried split peas along the seams!

7 Cover the cardboard with 3 layers of strips. Cut eyeholes in the cone with scissors.

8 Cut out a semicircle as shown, to allow the cone to fit around the chin and neck.

9 Make 2 holes at the top of the helmet. Thread the string through the holes and knot it.

MAKE A MOBILE

Papier-mâché shapes can be hung with thread from coat-hangers, or from bars made from dowels or balsa wood. Hang the mobile up near a door or window, where currents of air will make the shapes spin around.

1

Fold a piece of cardboard in half. Draw or trace 5 mobile shapes onto the cardboard, and cut out with scissors.

2

Staple the tops and sides, and stuff with tissue paper. Staple the gaps, and cover with 3 layers of pasted strips.

3

Paint and varnish in the usual way. When dry, thread the top of each shape using a needle.

4

Cut one length of balsa wood of 18 inches and two of 8 inches. Sandpaper until smooth, then paint and varnish. Make holes at each end with a needle.

5

Thread two mobiles onto each of the short bars, as shown. Tie a piece of thread to the middle of the bar, and move it up and down until it balances.

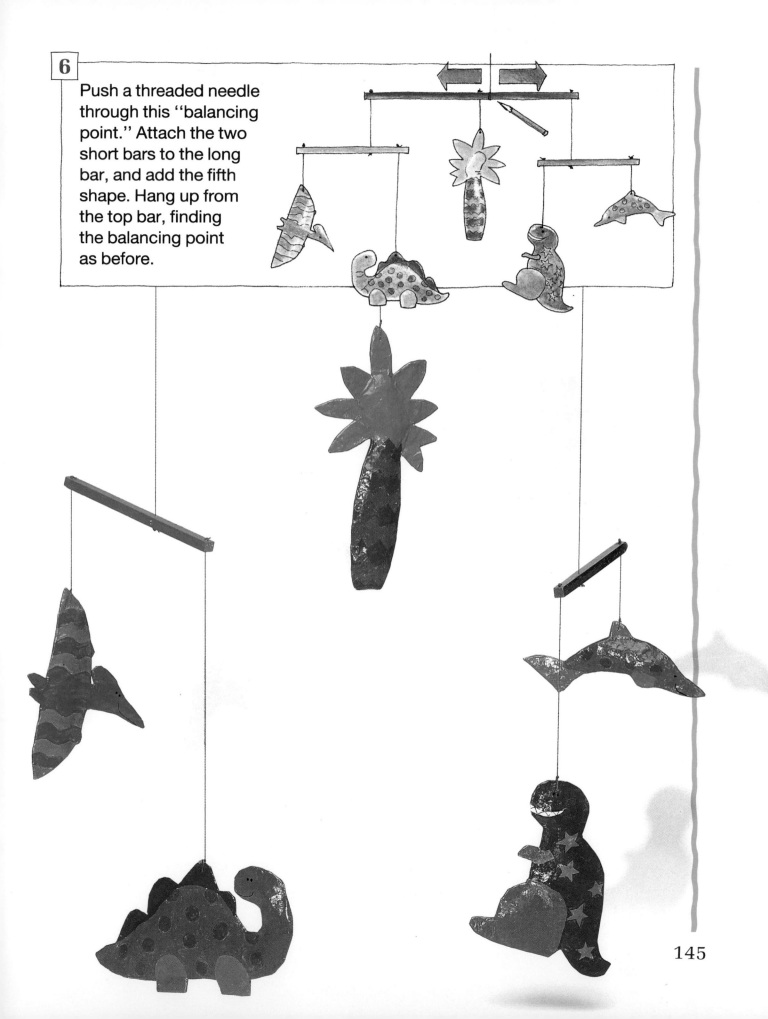

6 Push a threaded needle through this ''balancing point.'' Attach the two short bars to the long bar, and add the fifth shape. Hang up from the top bar, finding the balancing point as before.

145

PIRATE PUPPET

Here's a simple puppet that doesn't need wires or strings — just hold the body under the cloth and wiggle it around! First, blow up a round balloon and cover with six layers of paper.

Once you have mastered this basic shape, you can go on to design a whole theaterful of puppet characters!

1 Glue a cardboard roll to the neck. Cover with 3 layers of pasted strips.

2 Cut cardboard features. Glue to the face, and cover with 3 layers.

3 Mold ears and nose from pasted paper strips. Leave to dry.

4 Glue string to the puppet's head. When dry, tie a knot in the back with more string.

5 Cut the top off a plastic bottle, and push in the puppet's head. Glue to hold it.

6 Cut a cross in each side. Push through a piece of balsa wood, and glue in place.

7 Paint the head, and glue on a scrap of material for a headband. Add a gold earring, if you have one.

8 Dress in a child's (or doll's) T-shirt, or sew 2 T-shaped fabric pieces. Tie a bandanna around the neck.

9 Make two small gloves from scraps, as shown. Stuff with cotton and glue one to each of the wooden arms.

SPECIAL DAYS

Lightweight papier-mâché is great for making Christmas tree ornaments. Try using gold and silver paint and glitter pens to add some sparkle. On *page 150* you will find some ideas for celebrating Easter and Halloween.

A Christmas Angel

Cut wings out of cardboard. Cover with a thick layer of pulp (see page *125*). Lay a sheet of plastic wrap over the pulp, and roll lightly with a rolling pin. Trim the edges with a knife. Push a paper clip into the back, as shown, and leave to dry out. Mold the head from a ball of pulp. When dry, glue to the wings. Paint and varnish as usual.

Balls

Blow up a small round balloon, and cover with 6 layers of strips. When dry, burst the balloon, remove, and paper over the hole. Paint and varnish the balls, or glue on scraps of wrapping paper. Push a bent paper clip through the top, and glue in place.

Christmas Shapes

Cut Christmas shapes out of cardboard, and paper both sides with 3 layers of strips. Paint them and varnish as usual. Make a hole through the top and thread with ribbon.

Easter Egg

Cover an oval balloon with 7 layers of strips. When dry, ask an adult to cut it in half with a sharp knife. Glue a long strip of cardboard to the inside rim of one of the halves, and cover the rims of both halves with 2 layers of small strips. When dry, both halves should fit together as shown below. Paint and varnish the egg.

Halloween Pumpkin

Cover about $^3/_4$ of an oval balloon with 7 layers of strips. Leave to dry. Cut the top of the pumpkin into points with scissors, and ask an adult to cut out the eyes, nose, and mouth with a sharp knife. Paint bright orange on the outside, and black inside. Varnish, then thread each side with thick thread and hang up.

ROSE BOX

Shoe boxes, hatboxes, candy boxes — all these can be transformed by papier-mâché!

1. Draw around the box on thick cardboard. Add an extra $3/4$ inch all around, and cut out to make a base. Repeat to make a lid.

2. Cut a piece of cardboard, $1/3$ inch less wide and $1/3$ inch less long than the box. Glue this piece to the middle of the lid.

3. Glue the box to the middle of the base. Cover the box and lid with 3 layers of strips.

4. Add roses and leaves *(see page 130)* to the box. Paint and varnish.

UNUSUAL GIFTS

Museums and history books are a good source of ideas for papier-mâché. The shape of this object comes from a picture of an ancient Chinese burial urn!

1

2

3

1. Glue legs to a deep box — these are made by gluing thin cardboard rolls to the bottom. You could also make cone legs for the box, as shown on page 132.

2. Glue on handles made from folded cardboard.

3. Cover with 3 layers of strips, adding more around the tops of the legs. Paint and varnish.

Molds come in lots of different shapes and sizes. Use them to make great-looking lids for boxes.

1. Grease the inside of the mold with petroleum jelly. Press in a thick layer of paper pulp, and leave to dry.

2. Ease out of the mold. Draw around the outline on cardboard, cut out and glue to the bottom. Cover with two layers of strips.

3. Cut a strip of cardboard. Curl it into an oval shape, making it just smaller than the lid. The lid should be able to rest on the top. Tape firmly in place.

4. Cut a bottom for the box out of cardboard, and glue in place.

5. Cover both sides with three layers of strips. Paint and varnish.

153

JEWELRY

Because papier-mâché is so light, it can be used to make really large, dramatic pieces of jewelry. The metal attachments (called *findings*) can be bought quite cheaply from craft and hobby stores.

Earrings

Method 1. Cut shapes out of spare pieces of papier-mâché. For a raised surface, glue on a pattern made out of string, and cover with a layer of strips.

Method 2. Cover clay shapes with 6 layers of strips. When dry, take off and trim with scissors.

Glue studs to the back of the earrings, or push through earring hooks. Use tweezers for opening the links.

2

1

Beads

Cut lots of long, V-shaped strips of paper. Cover each strip with paste, and wrap around a knitting needle. Slip off, and leave to dry. Paint, varnish, and thread to make a necklace.

Bracelets

Cover an empty tape roll with 3 layers of strips. Add texture with glued-on dried pasta shells or string. Paint and varnish.

More Baubles

Make huge buttons from papier-mâché, or try decorating combs and barrettes. Use glitter for a sparkly effect — or cover the pieces with scraps of silk or tissue paper.

SPOTTED DOG

This dog's body is made from a large cardboard tube, and the legs are made from smaller tubes. Giraffes, zebras, lions, and tigers (in fact, any kind of animal you like) can all be made in a similar way.

1

Cut a small tube in half and glue together as shown. Cut the top of the tube diagonally.

2

Repeat with a second tube. Tape to one end of the large tube, to make the back legs.

3

Flatten both ends of two more small tubes. Tape them to the front end of the body.

4 Glue a yogurt container, or a cardboard cone, to the front of the tube. Cut a flap for the muzzle as shown, and glue to the head. Add ears made out of cardboard.

5 Cut small circles and glue under the back legs to make paws. Cover the dog with 4 layers of papier-mâché. Add extra strips around the joints and around the big tube to pad out the shape. Push in a tail made out of garden wire, and cover with 3 layers of strips. When dry, paint and varnish in the usual way.

MORE IDEAS

Try making some small toys from papier-mâché — mold the shapes from modeling clay and cover with six layers of tiny paper strips. When dry, cut in half and take off the mold. Glue the halves back together, and paint. Old bath toys, like the duck on the right, also make good molds...

For jointed toys (like the bear shown above on the left), make the limbs and the body separately. Link to the body with a needle threaded with elastic...

Use balloons and cardboard tubes to make maracas like the ones on the left! Fill with dried peas or beans...

Large cardboard boxes can be turned into fantasy buildings with papier-mâché. By adding "extras" — made with cardboard, you could make a castle, a garage, or even a whole dollhouse. Make furniture from tubes of cardboard, and other scraps.

MAKING
CARDS

WHAT YOU NEED

To make the cards in this book, collect together a basic kit like the one shown here. Some of the projects require a few extra bits and pieces—check by reading through the step-by-step instructions before you begin.

Glue

Scissors

The Basics

The main thing you'll need is a supply of thin cardboard. Heavy paper can also work well. If you use thin paper, fold each sheet in half to double the thickness—otherwise they'll be too floppy to stand up!

Colored tissue, crepe, wrapping paper, old magazines, and wallpaper can all be used to decorate your cards.

Felt-tip pens

Dried beans and lentils

Foam block

Square

Tools of the Trade

You'll need a pair of scissors, a square, a craft knife, a metal ruler, paintbrushes, pencils, and a cutting board to protect your table—a big piece of cardboard, wood, or Formica is ideal.

Always handle craft knives very carefully, and only use them when an adult is around to help.

Paints and Glue

For sticking paper and cardboard together, use ordinary white glue or paper paste.

Most of the cards in this book were decorated by cutting shapes out of paper and gluing them to the design. You could also color your cards with paints or felt-tip pens.

Paper and cardboard

Paper fasteners

Metal ruler

Colored pencils

Brushes

Craft knife

Bits and Pieces

Other useful materials include foam blocks for printing, a needle and thread, a rubber band, and paper fasteners.

Fabric scraps, felt, dried beans and lentils, aluminum foil, and any other bits and pieces can be used to make collage cards.

Poster paints

Aluminum foil

161

HINTS AND TIPS

The cards in this book are all easy to make—
they're also a lot more fun to send than ones
you've bought from a store! Just take your time,
and follow all the instructions carefully. Before
you start, read the tips below.

Measuring

It's best to use a square
rather than a ruler when
you're measuring your
cards. If you use the
right-angled edges to
help you draw the
corners, your cards
will look very
professional.

Folding

Folding cardboard is
easier if you *score* it
first. Measure and draw
the fold line using a
ruler and a pencil. Then
press the nib of an
empty ballpoint pen
along the line, using a
metal ruler as a guide.

Illustrating

To illustrate your cards,
you could simply paint
a design on the front.
Or, cut shapes from
colored paper and
glue them down. You
can even make collage
cards, using all kinds of
bits and pieces.

*The pictures on the right show three different
ways of illustrating the same design. Each
illustration was done on a separate piece of
cardboard, then cut and glued onto a piece of
folded cardboard. This is called "mounting."*

Painted card

Collage card,
made with felt,
beans, and seeds

Card decorated
with paper
shapes

PRINTING CARDS

Use small shapes to print borders. They are also a good way to build up pictures—for example, a simple oval shape was repeated to make the petals of the sunflower opposite.

1

Draw a simple shape onto a piece of thick Styrofoam using a felt-tip pen. Cut the shape out carefully with a craft knife.

2

Cut several squares from thin cardboard or construction paper, each a little smaller than the folded cards you have already prepared.

Printing is a quick way to make a big batch of cards—at Christmas, for example, or when you want to invite a lot of friends to a party. Before you start printing, cut out all the cards you need. Fold them in half and put them to one side.

3

Pour some poster paint into a saucer. Dip the printing shape into the paint and press it firmly onto one of the squares.

4

Keep dipping and printing until you have enough pictures. When they're dry, mount them onto the front of the folded cards.

MAKING ENVELOPES

Your cards will look extra special if you send them in your own homemade envelopes! The instructions given here will work for any size. Try printing the backs and borders with brightly colored paints *(see pages 164–165)* and sealing the flaps with glue or stickers.

1 Lay your folded card on a big sheet of colored paper. Draw around it, making the line ¼ inch wider on all sides.

Leave ¼ in. between card and line

2 Draw another rectangle under the first one. It should be exactly the same width, but about ¼ inch shorter.

Why send plain envelopes when printed ones look so terrific?

3 Draw curves inside the bottom two corners. Add two ¾-inch flaps at each side of the top rectangle, as shown.

4

Draw a triangle at the top, making it at least 2 inches deep so that it overlaps the bottom rectangle when folded.

5

Glue flaps

Cut out the shape with a craft knife. Fold all the lines inward, and glue the bottom rectangle over the side flaps.

167

BIRTHDAY SHAPES

Here are some very simple cards that just need a little folding and cutting. The colorful numbers would make great birthday cards for friends, brothers, or sisters—or how about making the leaping dolphin for an animal-loving mom or dad?

1 Folded edge

2

3

Number Cards

Draw a number onto a piece of folded cardboard. One side must touch the fold.

Cut out the number, making sure you don't cut through the folded part of the design.

Paint the card, or decorate it by gluing down shapes cut from colored paper.

Stand-ups

Cut out a rectangle from cardboard and lightly pencil a line across the middle.

Draw a design with the top part just above the middle line. Color with paints or paper collage.

Cut around the top part with a craft knife. Then score along the line and fold backward.

The train was made in the same way as the number cards, but the folded edge is at the top, not at the side.

The ark and dolphin both have a simple stand-up shape that can easily be cut out with a craft knife.

169

SURPRISE!

Always keep the main picture of a surprise card hidden—just hint at what's underneath, as we've done here with the tip of the tiger's ears!

1

5 in.

10 in.

Measure a 10 x 5-inch rectangle onto a piece of green cardboard and cut it out. Score a line down the middle and fold the card in half.

2

Draw a simple bush shape on the front of the card, as shown in the picture. Cut along this line, using a craft knife or scissors.

3

4

Close the card and lightly sketch the tip of the tiger's ears on the inside, using a pencil. Open the card again, and draw the rest of the tiger's body.

Use paints or pieces of colored paper to decorate the inside and outside of the card. Write your message on the back.

Secret Message

Cut a dog's body out of colored paper and glue it to the front of a folded piece of cardboard. Draw and cut out the dog's head, and glue just the top part to the card.

Make a tiny envelope *(pages 166–167)*, tuck in a secret message, and stick it under the dog's chin!

PUZZLE CARDS

The pictures on these cards are magically revealed when the pieces are put in the right order or when the dots are joined together!

1

2

Dot-to-Dot

Lightly draw a simple design onto a piece of paper, using a pencil.

Use a felt-tip pen to mark clear dots along the pencil line.

3

Number the dots in the correct order. Erase the pencil marks and mount the picture onto a card.

Jigsaw Card

1 Draw a rectangle measuring 7 x 6 inches onto a piece of cardboard. Cut it out.

2 Draw a border ¾ inch inside the edge of the cardboard. Cut along border to make a frame.

3 Place the frame on another piece of cardboard. Draw along the inside with a pencil, and cut this out.

4 Turn this piece of cardboard into a picture using paints or paper collage, then cut it into simple jigsaw pieces.

5 Fold a 12 x 7-inch piece of cardboard in half and glue the frame to the front. Send in an envelope, along with the jigsaw pieces.

POP-UP CARDS

These cards look terrific, and they're easy to make when you know how! You can change the picture to suit any kind of theme—just follow all the measurements given here.

1 Take two pieces of thin cardboard, each 12 x 6 inches. Score and fold both pieces of cardboard down the middle.

2 On one of the pieces, measure 2 inches along the fold from either edge, and mark the two points with a pencil.

3 Draw a 3-inch line through each of these points (1½ inches on either side of the fold). Cut along both lines.

4 Now lightly score two lines between the cut lines, as shown.

5 Close and open the card, making the center strip fold inward.

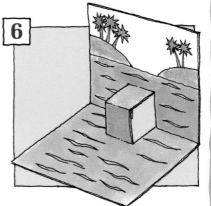

6 Decorate the background with paints or paper collage.

7 On a new piece of cardboard, draw a pop-up shape that will fit inside the card.

8 Cut out and decorate the pop-up shape. Glue it to the lower half of the center strip, as shown.

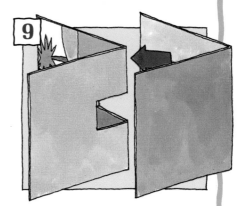

9 Glue the other piece of cardboard to the back —but don't put any glue on the center strip!

ZIGZAG CARDS

Fold, cut, and unfold—and a whole herd of elephants appears! Try cutting out a different design and you have a row of teddy bears, or a little train . . . .

The tomato card has a special surprise tucked into its front pocket—a pack of seeds that grow into beautiful plants!

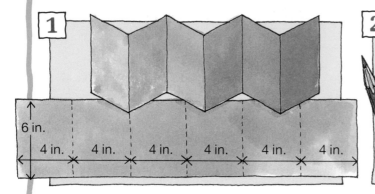

1

6 in.

4 in.   4 in.   4 in.   4 in.   4 in.   4 in.

Take a strip of thin cardboard, measuring 24 by 6 inches. Divide it into six 4-inch sections with a ruler and pencil. Score along the lines, then fold the card into a zigzag.

2

At least $\frac{1}{2}$ in.

Draw your design onto the front of the folded strip. Make sure the design touches both sides of the card for at least $\frac{1}{2}$ inch at each point, or it will all fall apart when you cut it out!

3

Cut out the design, then carefully unfold it again. Paint one side of the card, or glue down shapes cut from colored paper. Write your message on the back of the card.

Say It With Seeds!

Buy a pack of seeds. Cut and fold a zigzag (make it a little bigger than the pack). Cut a cardboard pocket for the seeds and glue it to the front.
   On the inside, show what happens when you plant the seeds!

TOMATO

MOBILES

Yet another brilliant idea that's a lot easier than it looks. This type of card is very eye-catching because the mobile shape keeps swinging around in even the gentlest breeze.

1 Cut out a rectangle of cardboard, and score a line down the middle. Draw a border on the front—the cards in the photo should give you some ideas.

2 Cut out the part inside the border and fold the card in half. Paint the front and insides of the card, or decorate them with paper shapes.

3 Cut out a shape from another piece of cardboard. Make sure that it fits within the border. Draw around it to make a second shape and cut this out, too.

4 Cut a piece of thread about 3 inches long. Tape it lightly to one of the shapes—alter the position until the shape balances from the thread.

5 Glue the second shape over the first so that the thread is trapped between them. Decorate both sides of the shape with paints or paper collage.

6 Tape the top of the thread inside the front of the card. Check that the shape can swing around without touching the border.

MOVING PICTURES

Pull the tab and watch the balloon glide across the sky! For this design, you'll need one piece of cardboard measuring 8 x 6 inches and another measuring $16\frac{1}{2}$ x $6\frac{1}{2}$ inches. You'll also need to cut out a narrow strip, 10 inches long and 1 inch wide.

1

Cut a curved slot in the smaller piece of cardboard using a saucer as a guide. Leave 1 inch on both edges.

2

Decorate this piece, avoiding the curve. Draw and decorate the balloon on another piece, and cut it out.

3

Cut the narrow strip into two pieces. Glue the pieces into an "L" shape, and tape over the corner.

4

When the glue is dry, tuck the shorter length of the "L" through the slot from behind, as shown in the picture.

5

Glue the balloon to the top of the "L" shape. Check that it moves freely when you pull the other end of the strip.

6

Fold the larger piece of cardboard, and glue the decorated piece to the front. Don't put glue near the "L" strip.

The winged horse flies across the sky in the same way as the balloon. You could also try drawing a bird, a plane . . . or even your favorite superhero!

CARDS WITH FEET!

These cute 3-D cards can be folded flat for sending. The methods shown here can be adapted to make animals of all shapes and sizes—how about a tall giraffe, a plump hippo, or even a whole team of reindeer for Christmas?

1

Body

Legs

Make two pairs!

Fold card in half and cut out this pattern.

2

Crocodile and Turtle

Draw the turtle or crocodile's body onto stiff cardboard, and cut it out. Make two pairs of legs as shown.

Cut two $\frac{1}{2}$-inch slots in the body, and one into the top of each pair of legs. Decorate, and slot in the legs.

1

At least $\frac{1}{2}$ in.

2

Fold over to make tail

Owl

Draw the body onto cardboard and cut it out. Cut a slot across the bottom half, leaving at least $\frac{1}{2}$ inch between the slot and each edge.

Cut out and fold a shape like the one above for the feet and tail. Slot this through the body. Decorate the owl using paints or paper collage.

Decorate one side of your animal card using paints or paper shapes. Then write your message on the other side—use a fountain pen, a colored felt-tip, or, best of all, a gold or silver pen.

WINDOW CARDS

"Stained glass" cards look beautiful and mysterious—they're often made at Christmastime, but there's nothing to stop you from sending them in spring, summer, or fall!

1 Cut out a 6¾-inch square of cardboard. Draw a design onto the front, leaving at least ¾ inch between it and the edge. Leave "bridges" of at least ⅓ inch between the holes.

"Bridges"

¾ in.

2 Cut out the holes for the "windowpanes" with a craft knife. If you cut through a bridge by mistake, fix it with tape.

Cut the windowpanes from pieces of colored tissue paper or crepe paper. Put glue on one side of the cardboard and stick down the colored pieces— trim them so they don't overlap.

Fold a $15\frac{1}{3}$ x $7\frac{3}{4}$-inch piece of cardboard in half. Draw a $\frac{3}{4}$-inch border onto the front and cut out the middle. Glue your stained glass window to the back, as shown.

ZODIAC COLLAGE

Most of the cards in this book were decorated by gluing down pieces of colored paper. However, you could also use old magazines, newspapers, aluminum foil, postcards, stamps, scraps of fabric or wallpaper, dried beans or pasta, flowers or grasses, shells, nuts and bolts . . . the possibilities are endless!

Here's how to make a zodiac card from collage. There is a design for every star sign! Copy the shapes onto cardboard, or ask an adult to enlarge them on a photocopier.

Cut and fold a piece of cardboard—as big or as little as you like. Draw one of the zodiac signs onto the front. If you're using a photocopy, cut it out and glue it down.

Sort out the materials you're going to use. Put glue on the design, a little at a time, and gradually cover it with your materials. Leave it to dry before sending.

Capricorn

Aquarius

Pisces

Aries

Taurus

Gemini

Cancer

Leo

Virgo

Libra

Scorpio

Sagittarius

CHRISTMAS CARDS

At Christmastime, when you need to make a big batch of cards, the best idea is to set up a printing press and go into mass-production!

For a few special people, try making the cat-in-a-stocking to hang on the tree—or turn the page to discover how to make a jolly Santa who jumps right out of the envelope!

Printed Cards

Follow the instructions for printing cards on pages *164–165*. Print simple shapes such as a tree, a present, or a star.

While your printing press is up and running, why not make your own wrapping paper—use wallpaper or brown wrapping paper.

Use scraps of cardboard for gift tags. Make holes with a hole punch, and thread with ribbon.

Christmas Cat

1 Fold a piece of thin, colored cardboard in half. Draw the stocking shape, with the folded edge as one side. Cut it out.

2 Glue the edges of the stocking together, but leave the top open. Draw and cut out a cat from black cardboard. Glue it in the stocking.

3 Decorate the card with bits of colored paper. Tape a loop of ribbon to the back, and write your Christmas greeting underneath.

All kinds of simple Christmas shapes can be used for your prints and tree decorations. How about stars, holly, snowpeople, or angels?

189

1

Pop-up Santa

Copy the diagram (shown right) onto a piece of red cardboard, using a pencil and ruler. Paint or decorate Santa's head and the chimney section.

2

Score and fold the cardboard in along the dotted lines, and tuck the Santa through the middle slit. The folded card should form a shape like the one shown in step 3.

3

DIAGRAM

Santa should be less than 3½ in. at widest point

Cut notches

5 in.

2 in.

2 in.

3 in.

½ in.

Middle slit

3½ in.

3 in.

Cut notches

2 in.

¾ in.

Loop one end of a rubber band over the notches at the back (A), and loop the opposite end over the notches at the bottom (B). This may look tricky, but it's very simple once you get the hang of it!

4

To put the card into the envelope, gently squeeze the sides until it is flat.

When someone opens the envelope, the rubber band makes the Santa pop back up!

VALENTINE'S DAY

Here's a stylish valentine to make for the one you love (don't forget to add your secret message on the back)!

Start by cutting out a rectangle of colored cardboard measuring 7 x 4¾ inches. Then cut out a square of cardboard in another color measuring 4¾ x 4¾ inches.

Try dangling a tiny heart on a piece of thread inside the main shape.

1

Score and fold the larger piece of cardboard down the middle. Then score a $\frac{1}{3}$-inch strip at each side and fold the strips toward you.

2

Fold the smaller piece in half. Draw a border $\frac{1}{3}$ inch from the edges. Draw half of a heart shape, making the sides touch the border.

3

Cut out the area around the heart or, for a slightly different card, just cut out the heart. Both types are shown in the photo.

4

Glue the sides of the card to the folded strips on the larger card. Leave to dry before folding again.

To make a pair of tiny hearts, just cut out a single heart from the middle of the folded smaller card.

EASTER CHICKS

When you open the top half of this Easter egg, a bright yellow chick hatches out!

You'll need cardboard measuring $4\frac{1}{3}$ x 3 inches for each egg, and a 4-inch square of yellow cardboard for the chick. You'll also need a paper fastener to hold the egg together.

1

Cut out an egg shape from colored cardboard. Cut a zigzag across the middle.

If fluffy chicks don't appeal, how about a baby dinosaur?

2

$1\frac{1}{5}$ in.

Place the top of the egg on the yellow square, and draw around it. Draw the chick inside the line, adding an extra $1\frac{1}{5}$ inch onto the bottom. Cut out the chick.

3

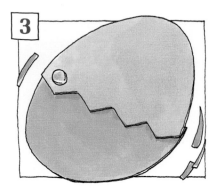

Overlap the two egg halves, and join them at one side with a paper fastener. Close the egg, and trim the edges to make a neat shape.

4

Glue the chick to the back of the bottom half of the egg. Cut out a strip of "grass," and glue this behind the bottom of the egg.

5

Cut and fold a $12\frac{1}{2}$ x $5\frac{1}{2}$-inch piece of cardboard. Glue the grass strip, the chick, and the bottom half of the egg to the front of the card.

Instead of step 5, you could make your egg stand up by itself—just glue a folded piece of cardboard to the back.

MORE IDEAS

You don't have to wait for a special occasion to send a card—it's a good way to keep in touch all year round!

Writing thank you letters doesn't have to be boring! Cut out a little card in the shape of the gift—then just scribble your note of thanks on the back.

Moving? Make some cards to let your friends know where your new home is!

Paper fastener

Pack some blank postcards and your paints or felt-tip pens next time you go on vacation—homemade postcards are a lot nicer than ones you can buy from souvenir shops!

MAKING BOOKS

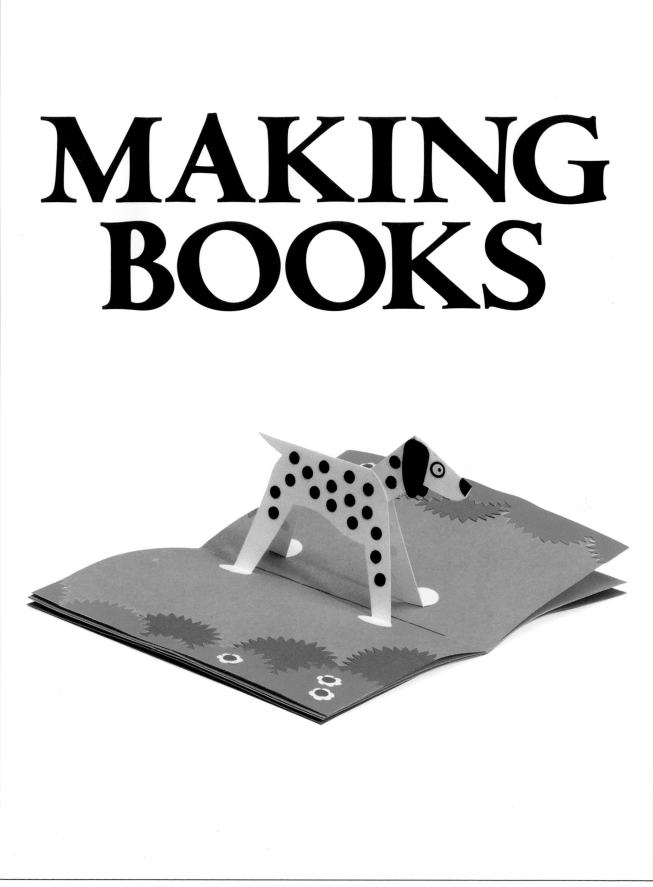

WHAT YOU NEED

First of all, you'll need to get together a basic bookmaker's kit like the one shown in the photo. You'll also need a thick piece of cardboard or masonite to protect your work surface from paint, cuts, and scratches.

Paper and Cardboard

You'll need plenty of thick paper or thin cardboard to make pages, and heavier board for hard covers.

Practice making books from scrap paper first. Then visit an art store to see the huge choice of paper and board available!

Glue

White glue or paste is good for sticking paper and cardboard together, and for making collages.

For more heavy-duty gluing (attaching a cover, for example), use safe household glues— *not* superglue.

Stapler

Bias tape

Glue

Craft knife

Scissors

Metal ruler

White glue

Ribbon

Tools of the Trade

To sew the pages of your books, you'll need a big darning needle, some strong thread, and a pair of scissors. A stapler can also be used to make some simple books.

You'll need a craft knife and a metal ruler to cut the cardboard and paper. *Always* make sure an adult is around to watch and help when you're doing any cutting.

Other Things

Among the other things you'll need are: poster paints, felt-tip pens, and colored pencils for coloring your books; strips of strong tape or bias binding for making hard covers; scraps of ribbon; colored fabric and paper; and a few large spring clips.

Poster paints

Strong thread

Paper and cardboard

Spring clip

Felt-tip pens

Pencils

Cotton binding

Brushes

String

MAKING BOOKS

The following pages show you how to make books of all shapes and sizes—just follow the step-by-step instructions carefully. Here are some tips on cutting and folding, along with some of the terms you'll meet throughout the book.

The *illustrations* are the pictures in your book.

A *spread* is two pages that face each other.

The *text* is all the words in the book.

The *heading* is usually bigger than the other words on the page.

Folding

Folding cardboard and thick paper is easier if you run a used-up ballpoint (or the back of your craft knife) lightly over the line first—this is called *scoring*.

Endpapers are stuck between the covers and the first and last pages of the book.

Spine

Front
cover

The *gutter* runs down
the middle of the spread.

*Although the books
shown on the following
pages come in many
different shapes and
sizes, the basic parts are
the same. These parts
are labeled here.*

Cutting

Craft knives are very
sharp and need to be
handled with care!
    Don't press too
hard—several light
strokes are best. A metal
ruler will help you to keep
the lines straight.

FOLDERS AND WALLETS

Folders and wallets have lots of different uses—unlike real books, you can change the contents as often as you like! You can also tuck in extra bits and pieces, such as maps, photos, magazine clippings—even a booklet or two.

1

2

Folder

Fold a big piece of fairly stiff cardboard in half (see the notes on folding and scoring *on page 200*).

Cut another piece slightly smaller than one half of the folder, and with flaps on two sides.

3

Cut several more pieces of cardboard, each smaller than the last. Fold the flaps and glue them inside the folder as shown. Leave to dry.

1

Fold along all 12 lines

2

Wallet

With a pencil and a ruler, copy the pattern shown above onto a sheet of thick paper or thin cardboard.

Cut it out, using a ruler and a craft knife. Score all the inside lines with an old ballpoint, or the back of the craft knife.

Fold along the lines. Make the middle fold first, then fold in the opposite direction along the two other folds.

3

Flaps

Glue

To finish your wallet, glue the top of the side flaps inside the bottom fold, as shown.

Left: A colorful selection of wallets and folders made from cardboard.

203

SEWING THE PAGES

The following pages show three different ways of sewing the pages of your book.

If you want to add a cover *(see pages 208–209)* to the books shown in methods A and B, you must strengthen the spine with a strip of cardboard. However, if you don't want a hard cover, you can leave this out.

Method A

Take up to six pieces of heavy paper or thin cardboard. Fold them in the middle, and stack them inside each other to make a book.

Cut a strip of cardboard the same length as your book. Trim the top and bottom diagonally, as shown, and fold around the spine of your book.

Strip of card to strengthen spine

Hold the pages of your book tightly in place with a spring clip. Then mark the middle point along the gutter with a ruler and pencil.

Add two more marks on each side of the middle mark, making them the same distance apart. Make a hole through the pencil marks with a darning needle.

Push the needle and thread through the middle mark, starting from the outside. Keep sewing in and out, following the direction shown above.

You should end up with two loose ends of thread outside the spine, as here. Tie them together with a double knot in the middle, and trim the ends with scissors.

Method B

Fold a big piece of paper in half several times (two folds make an 8-page book, three folds make a 16-page book, and four folds make 32 pages). Add a strip of cardboard along the spine as shown in step 2 of method A *(see page 205)*. Sew exactly as shown for method A. With a ruler and craft knife, neatly trim all the edges except the spine.

Method C

Take several sheets of paper of the same size, and stack them in a pile. Cut two cardboard covers and place them at the top and bottom of the pile. Hold everything in place with spring clips.

With a ruler and pencil, draw a line $1/4$ inch in from the spine. Mark five points along the line, all the same distance apart, and pierce them with a darning needle.

3

Thread the needle with strong thread. Sew around the spine in the direction shown in the picture.

4

Then sew back along the spine in the opposite direction. Tie the two loose ends together.

MAKING COVERS

The simplest kind of cover to make is a soft cardboard wrapper. However, if you want the book to be really strong and long-lasting, you could try gluing the pages into a hard cover, with a spine made from cotton binding or bias tape.

Wrapper Cover

Measure and cut out a piece of thick paper the same height as the pages of your book, but twice as wide, and with a wide flap at each end.

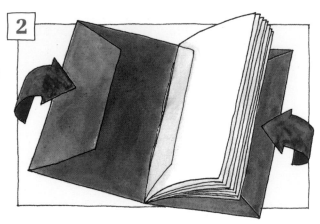

Trim the wrapper flaps top and bottom, then score and fold them in. Fold the wrapper in half, and lay the book inside.

Cut a flap in the middle of the front and back pages. Fold and tuck in the cover flaps, as shown.

Hard Cover

Cut out two pieces of strong cardboard. Make them about $\frac{3}{16}$ inch wider than the pages of your book on all sides.

Glue the pieces onto a strip of cloth, allowing an extra $1\frac{1}{2}$ inches at the top and bottom. Fold the extra pieces over and glue.

Cut two pieces of paper, 2 inches wider than the boards on the top, outer, and bottom edges. Trim the corners of the papers and glue to the boards as shown.

Glue the back of the piece of strengthening board to the cover. Then glue the first and last pages of the book to the inside of the covers. Or, cut two separate endpapers from colored paper and glue them between the cover and the book.

PRINTING PATTERNS

Try printing designs onto your covers—use poster paints for the stencils and printing blocks, and oil paints for marbling.

You can also make beautiful patterned endpapers in the same way, or even print directly onto the pages of your book.

Stenciling

Draw a design on stenciling board or ordinary thin cardboard. Carefully cut out the holes with a craft knife.

Hold the board down on the cover and dab thick poster paint over the holes with a piece of sponge or a stenciling brush.

Printing Blocks

Cut some shapes out of foam rubber and glue them to thick squares of wood or cardboard.

Dip the shapes into thick paint and press them down to print. When the paint is dry, you could add some extra details by using a darker color.

Marbling

Half-fill a wide tray with water. Mix some oil paint with mineral spirits until runny, then dribble them across the water.

Swirl the water gently with a clean brush, then lay a sheet of paper on top.

Smooth carefully, lift off, and leave to dry.

COLLAGE COVERS

Magazines, newspapers, and greeting cards can all be cut up and glued to your covers to make a collage. You can also use bits of junk to make pictures and patterns—they look best if you paint them afterward. A coat of clear varnish will stop the paint from rubbing off the covers.

Collage Castle

This castle was made from tree bark, aluminum foil, sandpaper, toothpicks, pencils, and bamboo— but you could use all kinds of spare junk! The moon was made from half a cashew nut.

Once the glue was dry, the castle was painted silver-gray.

Découpage

Cut pictures out of old wrapping paper, magazines, or news- papers, and glue them to your cover to make an overlapping pattern.

Look for interesting colors, pictures, and shades. Try tearing some of the pages—this gives a softer edge than cutting them.

Antique Book

Cut out some shapes from cardboard and some short lengths of string. Glue them to the cover in a pattern.

Brush black paint along the raised edges, then leave to dry. Rub gold paint over the cover with a dry brush.

BOOKMARKS

Make bookmarks from leftover cardboard! If your book has a theme, your bookmark could match it—for example, a monster bookmark could hang over the pages of a scary story!

Draw and cut a bookmark out of cardboard. Paint it, or decorate it by gluing on some cardboard shapes. Draw a flap and cut it out with a craft knife.

Slot the flap over a page in your book. You could also make a flap by gluing on an extra piece of cardboard (like the parrot's wing, see right)—only the top should be glued to the bookmark.

A Book Ribbon

Tuck a piece of ribbon between the piece of strengthening cardboard and the cloth spine before you glue them together—the ribbon should be about 2 inches longer than the length of the book.

These bookmarks come in all shapes and sizes—some hang over the pages by their paws, others by their tails, flippers, or wings!

DESIGNING BOOKS

Now that you've made your book, what are you going to do with it? You may want to use the book as a diary or a notebook, or to give it to someone as a gift. On the other hand, you could use it to write and illustrate a story, a poem, or anything else at all. Here's how you go about it.

Count how many pages you have in your book, then draw them on a piece of paper. This is called a *page plan*. It will help you to work out where you want your text and illustrations to go.

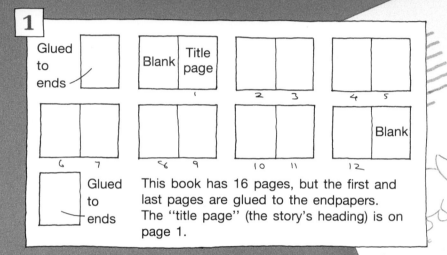

This book has 16 pages, but the first and last pages are glued to the endpapers. The "title page" (the story's heading) is on page 1.

Decide how many lines of text to put on each page. Some pages can have more text than others, as you can see from the designs shown here.

3 Plan where your text and illustrations will go.

4 Draw a writing guide on cardboard (the same size as a page from your book). Use a black pen, and keep the spaces between the lines equal.

Vary the position of the text and pictures—some ideas are shown here.

5 Write the words and pictures lightly in your book in pencil. Slip the writing guide under the page to help keep the lines of text even.

ADDING PICTURES

When you're happy with the way your designs look, you can use your pens and paints to fill in the words and pictures.

Do the illustrations first, using some of the suggestions on these pages. Then carefully write the words around the pictures.

The dinosaur spreads below were painted, while the planets and rockets were made by gluing on pieces of cardboard and paper.

The spread on the far right shows how magazines can be cut up and arranged to make collage pictures.

Painting

You can draw or paint the illustrations directly onto the pages. Or trace some pictures from your favorite books and magazines and color them in.

Paper Shapes

Cut shapes from cardboard or paper and glue them to the pages to make pictures (most of the photos in this book show books illustrated in this way).

Collage

Cut pictures from old color magazines and glue them into your book.

You could also use newspapers, photos you've taken yourself, or photocopies.

NOVELTY NOTEBOOKS

Notebooks can be quickly sewn or stapled to make presents for birthdays or Christmas—they can be any shape or size, as long as you remember to leave most of the folded edge uncut. You can either leave the insides blank, or write in special messages or information.

1 Fold several sheets of thick paper together. Draw on the design for your book, and sew down the middle of the pages *(see page 205)*.

2 Cut around the outline of the notebook as shown. Make sure you don't cut any of the thread that holds the spine of the book together.

3

Paint the front, or use some of the printing ideas *on page 211*. You could also glue on loops of cardboard to hold a pen or pencil.

Instead of sewing the books, you could staple along the spine—as we did to make the birthday cake book.

The snowman, elephant, and sunflower are all sewn. The birthday cake book is stapled down the side.

To make the butterfly, cut several wing-shaped pages and sew down the middle. Cut out the body separately, and glue it over the stitches.

ZIGZAG BOOKS

Zigzag books don't need any sewing! They can be written and read just like ordinary books, or unfolded and pinned to the wall to make a frieze.

These books look best if you make them out of heavy paper or thin cardboard.

Simple Zigzag

1 Divide a long strip of thin cardboard or thick paper into equal parts using a ruler and a pencil.

Fold the paper into a zigzag. Then add your illustrations and text (if any).

2 Decorate both sides—use them to make long, foldout friezes or to tell a story.

Two-color Zigzag

Take three sheets of paper in one color and three in another color. Fold them in half, and cut one of the pieces in two. Glue together to make a zigzag, with the two cut pieces at each end.

You could glue ribbon under the end pieces to tie up the zigzag, as shown.

POP-UP BOOKS

How about having pop-up pictures in your books? They look very impressive, but aren't that difficult to make. Like the flaps and moving parts on pages 227-230, pop-ups work best in books with fewer than ten pages made of thin cardboard.

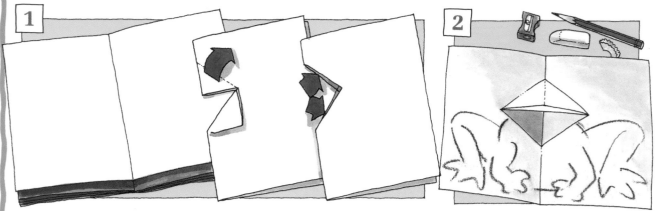

Mouths and Beaks

Cut a piece of cardboard the same size as a spread in your book. Fold the paper, and cut a slit near the middle. Fold back the flaps, and tuck in.

When you open the page, the flaps will open like a mouth or beak!

Color the picture, then glue the page into your book. Don't put any glue on the back of the mouth or beak.

Spirals

Draw a circle on some thin cardboard, slightly smaller than a page from your book. Draw a spiral inside the circle.

Draw a snake's head at the outer edge of the circle, as shown. Cut around all the lines with scissors.

Use paints, felt-tip pens, or bits of colored paper to decorate the snake and to make a colorful jungle background.

Glue the *back* of the snake's head to the right-hand page. Put a dab of glue on the *top* of its tail. Shut the book, press together, then open and leave to dry.

You can glue on extra details made from cardboard, such as this frog's bulging eyes!

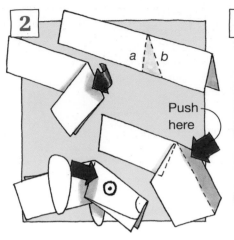

Stand-up Dog

Fold a 3 x 5½-inch piece of cardboard in half. Draw the shape of the dog's body and cut it out so that the folded edge is along the dog's back.

Fold a 1½ x 3½-inch piece of cardboard in half. Make folds *a* and *b*. Open and push down to make the head. Cut and glue on the ears.

Glue the neck into the body. Fold the paws back on one side, and glue the undersides to one of the pages, ½ inch from the gutter.

Fold back the paws on the other side. Dab the undersides with glue, and fold the facing page on top of them.

You can decorate your stand-up animals before gluing them into your book. This dog's spots were made with a hole-puncher and then glued to the body.

FLAPS AND MOVERS

You can add even more fun and excitement to your books by making flaps that open, holes to peek through, and wheels that turn! You could also use these methods to make really special greeting cards.

Flaps

Simple doors and windows can be glued straight into your book.

You can also cut flaps from a separate page of cardboard, and glue the page into the book.

Peepholes

Peepholes such as keyholes and window panes can be cut from the cover or inside pages to show part of the picture on the page underneath.

Mix and Match

Cut a small book into three sections. Draw a figure on the front. Open the flaps, and mark where the neck and legs join. Draw a new figure on each page.

Wheels

Cut out a cardboard wheel $\frac{3}{8}$-inch smaller than a page in your book.

Put the wheel on the page, and draw around it. Mark both centers.

Measure a $\frac{3}{8}$-inch circle around the mark on the page and cut it out.

Cut a semicircle from the page edge, and also from the page beneath it.

Cut out a window, leaving $\frac{3}{8}$ inch between the outer edge of the

circle and the window, and $\frac{3}{8}$-inch between the window and the center.

Draw a $\frac{3}{4}$-inch circle in the middle of the wheel, with a $\frac{3}{8}$-inch circle inside it. Cut and fold up flaps *a* and *b* as shown.

Lay the wheel under the page, and push the flaps through the hole. Turn the wheel around, and draw inside the window.

Glue the edges of the page to the one underneath. Then glue another small circle to the flaps— *not* to the page.

Your wheel could show ghosts in a haunted castle . . . or a changing view from a porthole!

Glue hubcaps to flaps

Moving Machines

Draw a machine onto a page in your book, or make the picture from shapes cut from cardboard. Draw the outline of a wheel, and cut a $\frac{3}{8}$-inch circle from the middle of the wheel.

Cut two cardboard wheels, one with flaps *(see page 228)*, and one with a $\frac{3}{8}$-inch hole in the center. Assemble as shown. Cut a hubcap from cardboard, and glue it onto the flaps.

You can join other moving parts in the same way. Just cut a hole in one of the parts, and flaps in the other. Slot together as shown, and cover with circles cut from cardboard.

PEEK-IN BOOKS

Here's a very special bookmaking project, and once again, it's much simpler than it looks! The book has five spreads, so if you want to use it for a story or a poem, you'll have to divide your text into five separate sections.

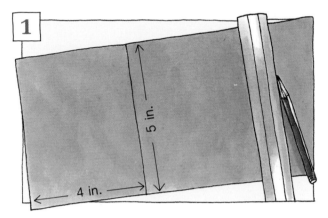

To make the background for the book, cut a strip of thin cardboard 5 x 40 inches. Use a ruler to divide it into ten pages, each 4 inches wide.

Cut a strip measuring 5 x 25 inches for the foreground. Allow a 1/2-inch flap at each end. Divide the rest of the strip into ten pages, each 2 1/2 inches wide .

Cut a slightly thicker piece of cardboard for the cover (5 3/8 x 9 1/4 inches). Measure a spine 1/2 inch wide down the middle and score along the lines.

Draw and color the five background spreads (each spread is made up of two pages). It's best to keep these pictures quite simple.

You can use paint to decorate the foreground and background, or glue shapes cut from cardboard, as shown here.

5

Plan illustrations for the five foreground spreads, allowing for peepholes in each one. Paint the spreads, or glue on cutout pictures.

6

Fold both the strips carefully into zig-zags, as shown above. Fold the two $\frac{1}{2}$-inch flaps at both ends of the foreground strip outward.

7 Put short lengths of ribbon between the cover and the first and last pages of the background strip, then glue the pages to the cover.

8 Put a thin line of glue down all the folded edges of the background strip and on the flaps of the foreground. Glue the two strips together.

Several books can be put into a box called a *slipcase*. Cut the case shape shown from cardboard, using the size of the books as a guide.

The length and width of the case should be about $1/2$ inch longer than the books, and the depth should be $1/2$ inch wider than the spines of the books when they're stacked together. Add flaps, fold up, and glue into a case.

Width

Length

Depth

Flaps

Slipcase

Scroll

Scrolls were among the earliest types of book. Make one by rolling up a sheet of paper and tying with ribbon—add a "seal" cut from cardboard, if you like.

Try gluing a magnet to the back of a tiny book, and sticking it on the fridge!

Fridge magnet notebook

INDEX